# MORE CLIENTS
# MORE OFTEN
# MORE MONEY

70 Strategies That Will Dramatically
Change The Way You Do Business

## Jim Gehrke

Illustrated by Olivia Gehrke

ISBN-13: 978-0692460719

ISBN-10: 0692460713

PRINTED IN THE UNITED STATES OF AMERICA

## Businesses I Have Helped

I have been a successful entrepreneur since 1994. When I met Jim, I was starting up a new business and I needed to fine tune it before I launched it.

Jim helped me answer some questions I had because I was "too Close" to my business. Jim helped me see things differently. It made a huge difference and a huge impact to my new business. I have been off and running ever since. Thanks Jim.

**Sonny Ahuja**
**Killing It Online**
**Sunny Ahuja.com**
**Atlanta, GA**

---

I have known Jim for a few years and I have to say that his insights and knowledge in the area of business growth and marketing have really helped me in my own consulting business and also my printing business.

There isn't a time I can remember that I couldn't turn to Jim and ask him about his thoughts on a business issue or a marketing situation I was having.

He has always been there whenever I have needed him.

**Pat Pendergast**
**Millennium Printing and Mail**
**Hartland, WI**

Jim you're a hardworking man who has survived the trenches of sales and self-employment. You have a great sense of humor and an approachable demeanor which makes you a great business coach.

You have helped me brainstorm through ideas and difficult situations. I love your approach of going back to the basics and get those correct before being enticed by the next shiny plan.

Any business who works with you will be happy with your customer service, follow-through and ability to go the extra mile in everything you do.

**Dana Johnson**
**Open Leaf Excursions LLC**
**Waukesha, WI**

---

"Jimbo you're the best. I can't tell you how much you've helped my business. You have given me the necessary direction and have prioritized my life in a way that fits my lifestyle which certainly is NOT cookie cutter. I wanted to balance my family and business life and you showed me how to do that. Thank you, Thank you, Thank you.

**Al McFadyen**
**BadAssConcrete.com**
**Germantown, WI**

# Dedication

This Book is Dedicated To My Beautiful Wife Kris Who Has Put Up With Me And My Shenanigans For These Many Years. I Love You So Very Much.

A Special Thank You Is In Order To My Friend **Kevin Kowalke** For Writing The Forward.

I Also Want To Give a Special Thank You To My Niece **Olivia Gehrke** Who Drew All Of My Illustrations. She Is a True Talent And Artist.

I Am Indebted To You All. Thank You.

And To Everyone Who Keeps Working Towards Their Dreams.

Continue On... Follow Your Heart And Aspire To Your Goals No Matter How Long It Takes You To Get There.

# Contents

# Forward

## By Kevin Kowalke

In business, the execution of one idea can change everything. Your business can go from struggling or mediocre to highly profitable and exciting. The key is your choice to take action.

In, *"More Clients...More Often...More Money,"* Jim Gehrke takes you on a journey filled with more ideas than you will ever be able to get around to doing. This book can become your go-to business-building guide from now until the end of your business career.

Jim has documented it all. You will explore topics such as, consistent lead generation, building trust, profitable pricing, effective selling, relationship building and so much more.

I have been asked by thousands of business professionals how to experience consistent growth while maintaining profitability and staying relevant. My answer to every person is you have to execute every day, every week, every month, all year for each and every year you plan to be in business.

I once asked a highly successful friend of mine what he believed was the difference between business professionals becoming millionaires versus those who never experience real financial success and his response was simple...

*"Execution. Hands down, those who will execute will have the fighting chance to bring to life all the dreams they ever had when it comes to business."*

I couldn't sum it up any better. That is why *"More Clients...More Often...More Money"* should become your reference guide to all things related to your business.

Jim has provided you a very comprehensive list of everything you should be thinking about when it comes to each phase of your customer life cycle.

I encourage you to only read this book until you find a "Big Idea," write it on a sheet of paper, then put down the book and go to work.

Take action on this one idea. Bring it to life. Create an incredible customer experience form it. Profit from it. Then come back to the book for another.

If you make that commitment and let Jim be your guide on your journey, you will find yourself with a business that will separate you from any of your competitors.

I encourage all of my clients to live by three simple words, and will ask the same of you, "Choose to Act!" If you declare this and incorporate it into your life every day, the results will be beyond your wildest dreams.

**Enjoy this comprehensive guide to business brilliance.**

# Introduction

Welcome to "More Client...More Often... More Money...". My name is Jim Gehrke President of Strategic Business Breakthroughs. I have had the fortune of consulting with many businesses over the years and I have found that when a business struggles it's very similar to how an athlete might struggle. When this happens, it's important to go back to the fundamentals or even develop them if you never did.

This program takes business fundamentals and kicks them up a few notches. Think of it as a second set of eyes or a coach just like the top-tier athletes have. Tiger Woods and Michael Jordan excelled because they had another set of eyes watching what they were doing. Their coaches were there for what they did right and wrong.

I have developed a plan to address these fundamentals and it focuses on the "3 ways to grow any business". You may have heard of this before, I certainly didn't invent it but I like to think that I defined it in greater detail than anyone else I have come across in my years of business.

Let me take a moment to tell you what the "3 ways" are and we can go from there.

1) Increase the number of clients/Leads you presently have

2) Increase the number of times a client visits your business/website

3) Increase the amount of money your client spends during each visit

I originally learned this strategy from business growth expert Jay Abraham. In fact he is one of my mentors so I borrow a lot of my strategies from him. He expanded this premise of the "3 ways to grow a business" into many specific action items you should implement in to your business.

I have expanded his list from his teachings to delve a little deeper into each of these three strategies.

Now to be fair, Jay wasn't the first marketer to use these three steps. Many marketers teach this but very few focus their business around these important strategies like I have. I have decided to do this because when you implement these strategies, your business will most likely double in sales.

I know that is a huge statement but when you realize the future potential of what your current business can become; doubling your sales may turn into tripling or quadrupling. I can say this because it's happened before; more than a few times.

Instead of me boasting about how much your business is going to grow; why don't we start into the program and you will see for yourself how much better your business will become if you implement these strategies.

So do me a favor; take a ton of notes and envision how you can implement each strategy into your business immediately. Don't wait until you read the entire book. That could be a delay of several weeks.

I have already taken the liberty of adding in a "Your Ideas" section after each strategy. Use that space to write your notes down. That way you never have to look for them and you have them right at the point when you were thinking of them.

I think it will be more powerful for you that way.

**P.S.** Not every strategy in this book is going to appeal to you or be the best use of your time. Start by doing those strategies that make the most sense to you and you can implement quickly.

The strategies that if you leverage correctly, will make the biggest impact on your business.

**P.P.S.** I hope you invested in this book to learn something you may not have heard before. I'm glad you have trusted me with this. I know you are person who takes action. Thank you. I will not waste your time.

**P.P.P.S.** One last thing. Look at the picture below. It's a business owner maybe much like yourself. I can confess that this has been me over the years.

If you're not sure what it is and what it represents just think of the famous saying that goes with this illustration:

## "Stepping Over Dollars To Pick Up Dimes"

Don't be this guy. Ever.

Ready???

Let's Go...

# Part One

# More Clients

This is the first of three overall strategies to grow your business. It is the one that every business focuses on the most.

It's the one that most businesses spend their entire advertising budget on. To many business owners; it's the one that they consider to be the life blood to their future existence.

It's important. Very important. But as you will learn, it's not any more important than the other two strategies. You see, to have a truly synergistic business, all three strategies need to be harmonious together. They need to be working like a well oiled machine. Think of a set of gears used in machinery Or a wheel that needs to be in round; no different.

With that said, you will notice that this strategy has by far the most amount of tactical steps that you can implement to increase the number of clients/leads into your business.

There are countless ways to bring in more clients/leads into your business. I hope this sparks a whole bunch of energy, excitement and countless thoughts on how you can implement this into your business.

I have listed 47 strategies on how to get more clients. I'm sure there are more but 47 should stretch your mind quite a bit. I already know your mind will explode with ideas you will come up with.

That's the fun part. The part of the process I never get sick of and you probably will be no different than me.

So let's go through the strategies and make notes. The strategies you love; do immediately. The strategies you're not sure of; put off for now. The strategies that you know you won't do; skip them all together.

What more clients will do for you is exponential. If you have 100 clients now and increase that to 120 clients with a couple of these strategies; you now have 20 more clients that you can enhance the quality of their lives.

You will also have access to their circle of influences who can refer clients to you. This alone will make the investment in this learning tool worth every penny.

The future is now. Have fun. Learn a lot.

# STRATEGY #1

## DEVELOP IRRESISTIBLE OFFERS

This may very well be the most important strategy. Irresistible offers give your clients a reason to spend their money with you. When a new client/lead visits your business, they are unsure, maybe tepid. Whether you know it or not, you are courting each other. It is your responsibility to make them feel comfortable with you. Build their trust with you.

An irresistible offer is an offer that is so good, so tempting that your client/lead cannot possibly say "no". It's a way to start a relationship together. A way to build trust. You probably know this already but the public is very skeptical of everything these days.

Think of an irresistible offer as a welcomed bribe so that you can show just how wonderful you are.

You will need to know what your lifetime value of a client is before you can make an irresistible offer. If you are bringing in clients at a discount which most of the time this is the case, wouldn't it be great to know that you can afford to do it?

Knowing the lifetime value of your client is critical to being in business anyway so you need to know this stuff. You need to know your numbers.

To figure this magic number, you will need to know how many active clients you have, how much they spend on average and for how long they stay as a client. Remember, these are averages.

Let's say your business has 275 active clients who spend $200 per year and stay for four years. Multiply 275 x 200 x 4. What do those numbers tell you?

You bring in $55,000 per year and $220,000 over the four years. Each client is worth $800 to you as their lifetime value. Remember these are averages. Some clients will spend less and others will spend much more.

Now you will be able to better determine what your irresistible offer can be.

## Here's an example:

You want to start running. You think about going to the local running shoe store and buy a pair of running shoes off the rack. You go there and find a pair you like and then one of their staff comes up to you and starts asking you questions about what it is you are looking for. In your mind, you already purchased the shoes you picked out but you play along with the sales clerk.

He asks you what your goals are, how long you will run for, where you will run, indoor or outdoor, how your feet are, etc...

This expert consultation gives you more knowledge about running that you ever thought was necessary. You quickly realized that the shoes you had picked out will not meet your needs but the shoes that are a perfect match for you are much more expensive and out of your budget.

Most people would leave and have to think about it because they wouldn't want to buy the inferior product now; that would embarrass them. The expert has an irresistible offer for their new client that he can pass along. He understands the new shoes are much more expensive and that he has given the new client so much information and education that any other shoe wouldn't do.

The store has an irresistible offer for new clients/leads where you get a shoe fitting for free ($49 value), you are tested on their treadmill to see your running form ($97 value), you will get a free membership to their running group which is perfect for you to continue your momentum into running and develop new friendships and you will also get a 15% discount on the shoes you will purchase that day.

The client has an offer they can't refuse. They spent more than they expected but they found a new home for all things running. Someone who wants the best for them... Someone who wants them to keep coming back time and again because they have taken the time to educate them. They were also educated on a new area of interest to them and they realized what they didn't know would hurt them.

## Call to Action:

First and foremost, figure out what your lifetime value of a client is. This number will dictate what you can and cannot do going forward as a business.

Once you have your lifetime value number you can  write down what you can give away to get a client. Also write down what you can't do or give away. This is a creative exercise.

When you create your irresistible offer, you will need to ask yourself if it's good enough to get you into the door if you were your own client.

Chances are you will most likely be your own worst critic so if it will convince you and you can afford to do it based on your lifetime value number then do it and own it.

Remember your offer can include bonuses like a FREE class or FREE report. It doesn't have to only be discounts. You have lots of options. Maybe it includes FREE stuff from a partnering business. Who knows until you start writing stuff on paper.

## Your Ideas

# STRATEGY #2

## PROVIDE GREAT CUSTOMER SERVICE

This may be the only place in this book where I use the term "customer". I use client because I believe a customer to be a nameless faceless soul.

A client is someone you cherish and would invite over to dinner. It might sound a little corny but for me it's a mindset belief that has served me well.

I know this sounds obvious but it needs to be repeated over and over again. In today's world we have social media that can instantly tell the world how you are doing. People love to talk about the good, the bad and the ugly in regards to their experiences.

One employee, one moment in time can make or break your business. Sounds dramatic but you all of had these experiences yourself when visiting other businesses in your life.

Providing great customer service takes a lot of work. It requires a tremendous amount of training and also a dedication to always do better than the day before.

It is important for a system to be developed that addresses customer service and its importance. There is no compromise here. It is very black and white.

I encourage you to try sales choreography. It is the art of the sale from start to finish. As soon as your prospect or client enters your world; what do they experience? Is it positive, negative or eh?

You want to control that entire process of your sales path. The online world does this masterfully because the human element is replaced with computer screens. Check out the sales process of a sophisticated sales company like Amazon.

They will walk you through the process one screen at a time and suggest things that may compliment the item you are looking at or have placed in your cart. They are there to help and to create another sale.

If you're a retailer you will want to pretend you're a customer entering your business. What do they see? What is their first movements? Are they led through a maze or can they roam free? When does an employee engage with them? Are they given a script to use or are they allowed to improvise the message? Is there a message or are they just saying "hello"?

Remember to put yourself in the shoes of a prospect or client? It will tell you a lot about your business.

## Here's an example:

You go into a restaurant that you were really looking forward to. It's one of the fancy places in your hometown. You are expecting a great meal and great service. Their reputation precedes them and tonight is the night.

Everything goes as plan, the servers are extraordinary, and they take care of your every need. They are professionals. The salad comes out at the perfect crispness, the table is set beautifully. They anticipate whatever you might need before you need it. Tonight you are royalty. You realize quickly that this is not your local chain restaurant that will hire anyone.

The kitchen however overcooked the steak and now there is a problem. The trained professionals you have serving you tonight never skip a beat. They have a new steak coming out to you promptly and your night moves on. You're thinking that they handled it exactly right but how could that happen? What you're not expecting is that they are going to buy you a dessert and give you a gift card for a future visit.

They will not take a chance that you will tell your friends about the steak. They also know that they value you as a client and anything other than a perfect night is unacceptable. They saved you as a client and they did it so seamlessly that it made you feel good about it.

## Call to Action:

I touched on this earlier but it needs repeating because most people give lip service to good customer service and do not make it a priority.

With that said, what can you do to make every prospect or client feel like they were welcomed, properly informed and treated like you would want to be treated. Remember the Golden Rule.

Go through your processes and write down what you do well and what you need to improve upon. It's important to recognize your strengths, it's not all about your areas of improvement.

Train your employees on exactly how you want your business to run. This is your business and your lively hood. This is not negotiable. You have to be very firm here because your employees are looking for a crack in your armor to slide right past.

So create your ideal client experience. Your clients are begging for it. They just haven't told you because they are used to something less than perfect. And that aint good.

## Your Ideas

# STRATEGY #3

## COMMUNICATE MORE EFFECTIVELY AND MORE OFTEN

Communication is completely in your control. That's the cool part because you can deliver a very specific message whenever you desire.

The key to this strategy is to deliver a consistent message and on a consistent time frame. Inconsistency is as good as doing nothing.

I know what you're thinking. You are afraid of bombarding your clients with too many messages. You see other companies do it and you hate that.

Have you ever noticed that those companies that you hate are only jamming sales messages down your throat? They are not giving you any valuable information.

Communicating more frequently by itself isn't necessarily the right way of doing things unless you include communicating more effectively. These two strategies are intertwined with each other.

### Here's an example:

There's a local women's boutique that has both home furnishings and clothing. The owner sends out three emails per week. Two of the emails offer either advice or how-to information i.e. how to fold a scarf for a certain look or how to place items on to a shelf for a nice look. The third email is an offer to purchase something that was featured in the emails.

The boutique also has a monthly newsletter for their clients that is mailed and emailed. Each quarter there is a postcard with that season's fashions and trends. They also have Pinterest, Facebook, Twitter and Instagram accounts for daily musings and inspiration.

Each communication continues to put the business at the forefront of their client's minds. If they need a new top or candle; who do you think they visit?

## Call to Action:

The best way to communicate more frequently and more effectively is to schedule your communication.

Create a marketing calendar where all of your communication is scheduled. Get a year-long calendar and mark down when your sales will be. When you will send out educational material. When you will send out your newsletter.

Don't worry about sending out too much material. If it has value to your client then they will embrace it.

Can you see where this will allow you to be more consistent with your message and be more effective?

## Your Ideas

# STRATEGY #4

## CREATE REFERRAL SYSTEMS

Referral systems are one of the top ways to increase the amount of new clients you reach. There are countless ways to start a referral system. A system can begin from one client. A client who refers so much business to you that you build a system around them. You can start a referral system around a group or club. Charities make for good referral prospects.

Here is a list of referral prospects for you to begin with. You will come up with many more as you spend some time on this because you never know where your clients come from until you pay attention to them.

- your current clients will be the best referral sources
- your vendors
- your business associates
- clubs you belong to
- your past clients
- clubs that your clients belong to
- referral contests work very well

## Here's an example:

A bowling alley wants to start a new league on Monday mornings for the third shifters and retirees. They can't afford traditional advertising so they enlist the help of their current bowlers. Remember... your current clients will be the best referral sources.

They ask all of the leagues if they know anyone who might want to bowl on Monday mornings. They offer coupons for FREE bowling for anyone who signs up as a result of their word of mouth. This is a perfect strategy for someone short on money. Keep in mind, most businesses never ask for referrals so they don't get many.

They presently have 500 bowlers who are potential referral sources. Besides the FREE bowling they offer a pizza party to the team who refers the most bowlers. At the end of the referral period, the bowling alley was able to put together a 6 team league on Monday mornings. That is 30 more bowlers who pay for bowling, buy drinks and eat food. Plus they might bring their friends and family in also to bowl sometimes.

Remember... You don't have to spend a lot of money to get a lot of help from your clients.

## Call to Action:

Create a list of all your potential referral sources. This will be bigger than you think it is.

Contact these referral sources and tell them what it is you would like to do. Keep in mind that not everyone will help you. That's ok. Your best clients, vendors, etc. will. They are your champions anyway.

Construct a message for each of your referral sources that is tailored to them. It could be the exact same message to each group but with a couple of changes like their name and their affiliations.

This is a strong strategy that will transform your business quickly and inexpensively.

As I wrote down the word "inexpensively", I realized that you can pay for the referral also. A small gift or a percentage of the sale in cash or company credit is also an option. You have to decide if this makes sense for you.

## Your Ideas

# STRATEGY #5

## ACQUIRE CLIENTS AT BREAK-EVEN OR BETTER

Sometimes you can sell things at cost or below cost if you know that your clients will spend money with you for a while or for much longer. A client's repeat purchase with you is considered the "back end" because they came back for more of what you offer. Real money to your business comes from the repeat sales of your products and services to your clients. Sounds a little confusing but you will see it very clearly in a second.

You need to immediately figure out what your lifetime value of a client is. That is the amount of money each client spends with your business and for how long they stay a client. I know each client has a different value but we are looking for the average of what your clients spend.

Let's say you have 100 clients who spend on average $200 per year with you. They stay with you for 5 years on average. That means every client you have will spend $1000 with you during their lifetime. The numbers do not lie.

What do the numbers mean to you in this example? Let's break it down a little further. It also gives you an idea of how much you can spend to acquire your clients. If you have, say, a 50% profit margin on your goods and services; you will make $500 profit on each client. So how much can you spend to acquire each and every one of your clients? Will you spend $5, $50, $100 etc.?

Have you thought about this before? Do me a favor... Go through your numbers and find out what your lifetime value is. You should have done this already.

## Here's an example:

A local jeweler gives away a heart shaped pin at Valentine's Day with any purchase. The pin has a retail value of $49 and they do display these pins at $49 every day of the week.

The jewelry store understands their lifetime value of a client to be $1750. Again this means that anytime they get a client to start a relationship with them and spend their hard earned money with them; each of their clients will average $1750 before they end their relationship with the jewelry store.

Keep in mind that the most common reasons why a client stops visiting your store is that they moved away, stopped needing your product or services or the biggest reason of the three is that you stopped paying attention to them and forgot about them so they forgot about you.

So with the knowledge of each client being worth $1750, the jewelry store has the means to give away a lot of pins. Quite honestly, with the markups that are common at jewelry stores; they probably can give away a free pin and still make money on the transaction. If they could do this then it would certainly be a win-win for all involved.

You're probably thinking that if you give away something of value, you will be taken advantage of by your new clients. They're called cherry pickers. I know this is hard but you need to not worry about them. They will most likely never be loyal clients of yours. Treat them with respect like your best client because you never know who they will tell about your business. They may end up as great referral sources for you.

## Call to Action:

I will mention the lifetime value of a client a few more times in this book. It is that important. You need to know your numbers as a business owner.

There is no shame in not knowing it before you read this learning tool because you probably weren't aware of it. Now you are so go ahead and get your client value. It will shock you what it is. I hope in a good way but if it's not good then we can raise it right now by implementing these strategies.

So, what does your backend look like? LOL

I hope that you have plenty of items that you can offer your clients to keep them coming back. If you don't create some items that you think your clients will like and want to buy.

This is about continuing on your relationship with your client. You want to be in a lifelong partnership together.

## Your Ideas

# STRATEGY #6

## OFFER STRONG GUARANTEES

Guarantees allow for new clients to try you before they get too invested in a new company. The public is very skeptical of businesses and they need to warm up to them. Offering strong guarantees is the best way to start a new beginning.

The longer the guarantee the more comfortable your client is. Craftsman tools have a lifetime guarantee. I have a few of them because of the guarantee alone. Lifetime is the best guarantee you can offer.

Guarantees and return policies scare business owners. They think the public will take advantage of them with this type of guarantee. This is bad thinking.

How many times have you returned something the last day you could because the receipt said you had 10 days to do it by? I know I have.

If that business would've put a longer time on the receipt I probably would've kept it because I would have forgotten about the return policy.

Do not let a couple of your clients who may abuse your return policies or your guarantees let you dictate a bad business decision.

They really aren't your clients anyway. They're probably cherry pickers and you shouldn't waste your time with them.

## Here's an example:

The local auto mechanic offers a spring tune-up for $99. This is a good deal for everyone involved. Good deal for the auto mechanic, good deal for the clients and a good deal for your car.

What the mechanic also offers is that, if for any reason your car has mechanical issues related to the tune-up within 90 days of service, we will service your car for FREE. Now that is a great guarantee.

If you are a current client, you appreciate the fact that your mechanic takes pride in their work and offers you a great deal. If you are a new client this gives you a chance to try out the mechanic before you decide if you like them or not.

## Call to Action:

How long of a guarantee can you offer? How strong of a guarantee can you offer? Write down what you can do and what it would look like if you doubled it.

What does that mean by doubling it? Can you extend your warranty or guarantee by twice as much time? Two years instead of One? Can you offer double your money back if not completely satisfied?

Interesting questions aren't they? Gets you thinking. How many of my clients would actually take me up on my guarantee? 1%, 5%, 10% or more?

It's been proven over and over and in every possible industry. The stronger your guarantee, return policy or warranty you offer the more sales you will enjoy and the less returns you will have.

I am assuming of course that you offer a quality product or service and that you are not a conman.

## Your Ideas

# STRATEGY #7

## PRE-QUALIFY YOUR LEADS UP FRONT

Only the very best sales companies qualify their leads up front. This means that not everyone who calls into your business is serious or someone you should pursue as a client. I bet that sounds weird huh?

Well if you ever chased a tire kicker for hours, days or months you know just how frustrating they are. For some reason a prospect who keeps saying "maybe" to you is encouraging. Instead you should run from them and cross them off your list.

Pre-qualifying a prospect is as simple as asking them leading questions to get them into a buying frame of mind. Things like getting a color choice from them or a timeframe when they might make a decision. Also ask why they are calling, their answers will tell you a lot about their journey to you.

### Here's an example:

The local auto dealership has an annual event for their anniversary. It is their biggest event. They have prospects coming and going all day long. They need to decide in a few minutes if a prospect is going to buy or just look.

It takes a delicate balance to know if a prospect is going to buy or not. A test drive is great sign of the start of a buying decision. If they pick a color; that too is a sign. When they pick out the options, you are home free. They are buying.

There will be dozens of prospects that will be browsing because they want to look at three or four different cars in the same category. They are shopping and don't want to engage with the sales staff.

It's the salesman's job to help them make a buying decision. Hopefully with them that day but chances are slim especially if they aren't ready to buy. You need to recognize that and get their information and move on.

One thing I want to mention that I haven't touched on is that even though you need to move on from tire kickers as quick as possible; it's also important to follow up with them. You see it requires a delicate balance to know when to politely excuse yourself from the sales process and when to push forward and close the sale. But always get their contact information so you can follow up with them on a scheduled basis.

## Call to Action:

A lot of the time pre-qualifying your prospects is over the phone or in an email. A prospect doesn't want to get themselves in a situation where they will have to make a buying decision.

This is frustrating for a business that isn't skilled at recognizing who they are communicating with.

So when pre-qualifying your prospects, you will want to create a sales script for you and your employees to walk a prospect through the sales process.

It's important to not spook them however and lose them forever so be careful. Your script will most likely need to be tweaked over time so don't worry about getting it right the first time.

A great way to do this, is by putting together a list of questions that will lead your prospect towards a buying decision.

Questions like:

--How did you hear about us?

--What type of problem are you having?

--How soon are looking for this?

--What is your time frame for your project?

--Have you done a lot of research on this?

You get the idea. Each question gives you a clue as to where your prospect is in their buying cycle.

If they are just starting out, you have the opportunity to be their mentor or supplier or reference source.

If they are seasoned and knowledgeable they may just be shopping price because they feel your product is no different than anyone else's.

This is tough for retailers who sell the same exact product. You will have to differentiate yourself from your competition so that it isn't just about price.

## Your Ideas

# STRATEGY #8

## CREATE JOINT VENTURES

Joint ventures (JV) are what could be one of your strongest strategies. A joint venture is when you work with another business to offer something to their clients that helps everyone involved. Consider it a partnership.

It helps your business because you get more exposure and hopefully a new client. It helps the business that offered your product or service because it gave something of value to their clients. Lastly it helped the client because they either wanted or needed the product or service that you offered them.

A true win-win-win. Something that we all as entrepreneurs and business people strive for.

Remember you are taking their clients and turning them into yours as well so please be respectful.

It also works the other way around. You can offer up your clients to someone else's business so that they can grow.

It is important that in either case, each business is satisfactorily benefited. It could be with a percentage of the sales which is common or with whatever means you can agree on.

## Here's an example:

A golf pro shop who offers high end golf clubs and accessories has struck a deal with the golf course around the corner from them. You get 2 FREE rounds of golf with every golf club set that is purchased.

The golf course is one of the nicest in the area so the value of the 2 FREE rounds of golf is $179 which is real money because that is what you would spend if you went there. The course is looking for new clients and the FREE golf gives the course the exposure they need and hopefully some sales in the restaurant and golf shop also.

The golf course would like more golfers because if a tee time passes and it isn't full with golfers then the course has lost revenue from that tee time. So the course gives the pro shop FREE passes to give away to their best clients knowing that if they've spent $700-1000 on new clubs they would be the golf courses target market for new clients.

The pro shop also wanted to give a great incentive to their clients for them to buy now that doesn't include dropping their prices and profit margins. The pro shop looks like the hero to their clients by giving them free golf. Besides when you buy new clubs, the first thing you want to do is hit golf balls with them.

## Call to Action:

Search out businesses that make sense to you and would make sense to your clients. In the example, I stayed within the same industry. This doesn't need to be the case.

You can search for items that your clients will purchase anyway like if you are a high end car dealer, a boat dealership would be a nice tie in. Or maybe a country club or a jewelry store. Go to where your clients already go.

Create your list and start contacting them. They need clients also. Make it a win-win-win and you can't go wrong. If the JV doesn't have your vision and can't see the opportunity then move on. Most people won't because this is a foreign idea to them.

If necessary, you can educate them if you really believe that they are the best fit for you.

## Your Ideas

_____

_____

_____

_____

_____

_____

_____

_____

_____

_____

_____

_____

_____

# STRATEGY #9

## LEVERAGE YOUR ADVERTISING

Being able to advertise your products or services is a great way to increase your business in a relatively quick time. There are different forms of advertising to consider. TV, radio, newspaper, magazine, internet, banner ads, billboards, etc.

The trick with advertising is that it has to give the prospect a reason to act... a reason why. Most advertising is about the business that is advertising and very self-centered. If it isn't client focused it will be a complete waste of money and you will leave with the feeling that advertising doesn't work.

In advertising there is direct response and image advertising. Image advertising is what you see in a magazine where there's the company name listed with a photo of a hot model. The problem is that the hot model is trying to sell perfume and she is just sitting there letting you believe that you too will be as cool as the model if you buy this perfume.

Direct response advertising is much more involved. It includes photos that only make sense to the advertising. It also includes a lot of words. Words sell. It's considered salesmanship in print and it's meant to tell a story. A story is a way to let your prospects know more about you and your products and services. It's a way for them to get to know you and your business a little before they engage with you.

## Here's an example:

I have a company that sells and installs backyard putting greens. I have tried many methods of advertising to bring in leads like radio, postcards and magazine ads.

The magazine ad was an image ad. Against my better judgment I took the advice of a graphic artist to make my ad "pretty". "Pretty" meant that it would have photos, my company name with contact information but nothing else. These ads ran twice and I received a total of zero leads from my "pretty" ads. 0 for 1

I also ran radio station spots. I ran these because I wanted the commercial to play at my tradeshows. I purchased several spots and they ran as planned. I received zero leads. 0 for 2

I also tried sending postcards to a targeted list. The postcard was a combination of photos and "reason why" text. I received five leads from the postcards. 1 for 3

There's something that needs to be said about what I chose for my advertising vehicles. I know my lifetime value of my clients to be $4875. I also know the profit margin of my business. I have the ability to spend a lot of money on advertising and still make a profit on the advertising spend.

The magazine ad was to a targeted group of golfers but it was an image ad and even though the imagery was on target, there was no message. It's vitally important to have a message. There was nothing to get people to call me or email me.

The radio spots were not to a target audience. They went to anyone who listens to that station. And if you didn't listen in that 30 sec. spot then it was missed forever. I figured it wasn't the best use of my money but I wanted that commercial for my tradeshows. I play it during the run of the show and it gets the attention of everyone around my booth.

The postcards went out to about 2000 high end homeowner golfers. I received five leads and those five leads resulted in one sale. I'm sure most of you are thinking that one sale out of 2000 postcards is a failure but that mailing cost me $915 with postage, printing and design. I made over $2100 on that green. I cash flowed just shy of $1200 on that mailing. Now it was worth it... wasn't it?

## Call to Action:

Figure out if advertising is for you. Take the costs involved out of it for a minute. Advertising should be an investment anyway not an expense.

Dan Kennedy talks about "message to market to media match". This is what you should write down before you figure things out.

Let's go through what Dan means by this.

Message - What do you have to say? What you will tell them? What are they looking for? How can you help them?

Market - This is your target market. Who are they? What are their interests? Is there an age, race, gender, geographic or economic bias?

Media - Where are they? How do they gather their information? Do they read, listen, watch or engage?

When you put these three things together you have a match.

Write down the different media you think might work for you and the target audience you are looking for. Try to narrow down the match as close as you can. Does the message fit the media you are targeting?

You wouldn't have an ad for Medicare on Facebook or in a skate boarding magazine. You might want to have an ad for a high end entertainment system in the Robb Report.

## Your Ideas

# STRATEGY #10

## DEVELOP STRATEGIC ALLIANCES

This is a strategy that will put you head and shoulders above your competitors. Some consider this similar to a joint venture but there are subtle nuances to strategic alliances.

This is more about networking with people who can help your business. Either they have knowledge you need or products you need. The most important asset I feel they have is their clients.

Affinity groups are an awesome place to look. Those are groups who form around something or someone. Fan clubs are affinity groups. Having the Green Bay Packers helmet on your license plate or credit card is also a form of an affinity group. The sierra club is an affinity group. I think you get the idea.

Their clients are the prize. Some businesses will just allow you to poach them because they don't understand the value of a client. Others will protect their clients as if their lives depended on it. Like you do... right?

### Here's an example:

Jay Abraham is one of the most brilliant marketers in the world. He feels if you have no other strategy besides forming strategic alliances, he could still make millions of dollars a year.

He had a company he was consulting for called "Icy Hot". Icy Hot had a great product but the company didn't have good distribution. Jay convinced them to advertise on the radio as their distribution source.

The owner of Icy Hot convinced Jay that if someone tries it, they will continue to buy it. So Jay came up with the idea of placing radio spots all over the country with any radio station that took their deal.

They gave the radio stations 100% of the sale for every jar sold. The company sold each jar for $3. The cost of the product was 45¢ to make and mail out so they money on each and every sale.

Icy Hot's money was on the back-end and they made millions of dollars with this technique.

The radio stations listeners are who Jay and Icy Hot wanted. They created strategic alliances with the program directors at radio stations across the country.

Are you thinking why would I sell something and lose money? Well, if you remember another strategy we talked about earlier, their money was going to be made on the back-end or repeat sales. The owner knew that those suffering from arthritis would buy at least 6 jars per year.

Another benefit was the mailing list the radio stations gave them of clients who have paid. They could now market directly to their clients.

At the end of the day, the radio station loved this promotion because they made money on each spot they ran through sales.

Icy Hot loved it because their advertising cost was FREE because they were able to absorb the loss on every sale. In fact they made money on each sale because of the lifetime value of a client.

Are you seeing how a lot of these strategies are tied in to one another? Very powerful when you combine them.

## Call to Action:

What can you do to create one strategic alliance today or this week?

Start a list of what you do that other businesses can benefit from. Maybe you have a great distribution channel that other companies would give a kidney for. How can you help them and help yourself?

Start another list for businesses that have something that they do well. Can it be integrated into your business for you to grow?

This is a pen and paper type of exercise that is very creative. Look outside of your industry as well. There are a lot of talented business owners who have figured out how to be exceptional at something who also don't know how to monetize what they developed.

That's where you come in. Be on the lookout for opportunities. Check out businesses you visit or see on TV, listen to on the radio, or read in a publication. Maybe a friend will know of someone or something and can refer you.

## Your Ideas

# STRATEGY #11

## DEVELOP YOUR OWN WEBSITE

The internet is stronger than ever and will get stronger each year to come. I know that's stating the obvious. It is amazing how the internet has grown over the last 20 years. It has gone from a few websites to everyone from the ages of 5 to 95 being on the web.

If you have a business you need to have a website. Even if it is a glorified business card. It gives you the credibility you need to show your clients that you are a real person. People trust people much more than businesses.

Websites do a lot of things for you and your clients. They do the simplest things like state your address and business hours. Give people your phone number or email address.

The best use of your website though is to educate your clients before engaging with you. Whether it is a video or several videos; it's important to start a relationship with your prospects to build trust. I know I bring up trust a lot but that is the world we live in today.

Websites also sell things. You've probably heard of Amazon, Ebay or a thousand others. Getting a website to convert sales is an art form. Companies spend thousands and some spend millions of dollars to convert these sales. For some companies a website is their sales staff.

Billions are spent on the internet each and every year. Grab a slice for yourself. Keep in mind that the internet is ever changing and you will have to keep up with it. It's not meant to scare you just something to be aware of.

## Here's an example:

The florist never had a website. She would rely on her walk-ins, weddings and other strategic partners she had lined up to give her business. She never thought she needed one because she always had clients. What she didn't know is that she was losing a lot of potential business because only the locals knew her.

What she needed in today's world was a website to capture the clients she was losing. Out of town clients sending flowers for a funeral, wedding, business or any other congratulatory reason.

Websites are the future of business even for the local mom and pops now. After the florist implemented a website, sales increased by 11%. It was a vehicle to show off her creations. All of the different arrangements she has made is now on the website so prospects can view her beautiful work.

## Call to Action:

It's easier to find something you like versus recreating it. Websites are no different. Find a website you like and model it.

Chances are good that it is a template and can be recreated in your business. Just to be clear, do not copy their site. Just model it.

Start creating your pages one at a time. Before you know it. Your site will be done. Maybe not put together but at least all assembled.

Hire a professional to put it together for you so it looks good and it looks professional. You want this to be the image of your business. They can do it quickly and most importantly get it done.

## Your Ideas

# STRATEGY #12

## LEVERAGE PUBLIC RELATIONS (PR)

Public Relations or PR for short can be the quickest way to boost your business. PR is the way to get the media involved to help them create and share a story. In today's world there is a 24hr news cycle that craves stories.

What is important to realize is that the media needs you just as bad as you need them. Whether it is the radio, TV, newspaper, magazine, online site or another companies newsletter; there's opportunity for you and your business to get recognized.

The power of getting PR is that you get an implied endorsement from that media. Even though they are not specifically endorsing you they are implying that they endorse you by spotlighting you. It's a perfect partnership for the both of you.

Start by writing a press release to send out to your local media sources. Find out who you need to contact at the local radio station, TV station, print media, etc. It's usually the producers of the different programs that you need to talk to. Send your releases to specific people and not to a generic address if possible. It's important to still send it if you can't get a name.

You have to be willing to be interviewed for the stories these different media sources will bring you. You might even become a celebrity in your own area or own business niche.

## Here's an example:

Sally is a life coach who would like more clients and more notoriety. She feels that if she gets interviewed on TV or radio, she will accomplish her goal. What Sally has to figure out is how she can help out the media. Remember she has to help them to help her.

There was just a huge layoff in the city Sally lives in. She knows that her guidance with this delicate situation will be very beneficial. She sends in a press release to the producers of the morning TV and radio shows.

The press release deals with the loss of a job and how to rebound from that. It deals with getting yourself back in the workforce after a devastating loss. It was timely to the needs of the stations and to the public she can help.

Sally went on two radio stations and one TV station. She is getting the recognition she wants for her business. If she continues she will be the go to person for dealing with stressful situations. The stations will call her first for her expert opinion. She will be able to raise her fees as her celebrity gains.

Having Sally on gave the stations the opportunity to show the public just how compassionate they can be. It made them look like they cared for their viewer. I don't mean to come off like these stations don't care because they do care. I was just trying to show that they have an agenda and they need you.

## Call to Action:

You may not have realized yet but many of these strategies can be borrowed from others who are doing well at it.

PR is no different. Look for examples that can be re-written for your business and turned into a successful campaign.

The headline of the Press Release is the most important part of the statement next to your contact info. Write out several different headlines that gets your message read.

By writing several headlines, it will open up your imagination to all of the different things you may want to say. It might also allow you to fine tune your message.

Keep in mind that you can't break the Cardinal Rule of Press Releases. The statement must be about the benefit to the media person you are sending this to.

What does this mean? If it only touts you and your business, it will go straight into the trash can. The media isn't interested into giving you FREE press.

They want to tell a story that benefits them. If you can help with the story then they will be interested. Not the other way around. They hold the cards.

So, write out how you can benefit them and use that as your strategy. Simple if you give it a few minutes. Use current events first and then trends.

## Your Ideas

# STRATEGY #13

## LEVERAGE SOCIAL MEDIA

Facebook, Twitter, Instagram, LinkedIn, Pinterest and YouTube are today's way of getting your message out. Most people use these for fun. To share their lives. Smart businesses use these techniques to make money.

Individual people make up your prospect and client lists. Social media is where individuals come out to play. It's where they review businesses both good and bad. People like to exercise their opinions using social media.

Social media is here to stay. I would suggest embracing it because you can really create a bond with your clients. An important bond that will only grow as time goes on.

Most social media is fairly easy to use. It is as easy as sharing words, photos and videos with an occasional offer mixed in.

Facebook - The King of all social media where it seems everyone in the world has an account. You can have a personal page for your friends and a business page for your business. It's free to join. Once you join it is all about requesting friends.

Post what's going on in your life. Post videos or pictures for your friends to see. There is no limit to the amount of words you can use.

A page is where you promote your business or service and you convince your friends to like your page. From there you post the information you want to get out to your clients and friends.

Go to Facebook.com and signup for your free account

Twitter – This seems to have resonated with celebrities and the media. Anyone can follow anyone with the chance to communicate with someone that they might not be able to in a traditional setting.

You are limited to 144 characters or less per tweet. You have to be short and sweet with your words. You can add photos, links and the all important Re-tweet.

Re-tweeting is where you take someone else's post and share it with your followers. It might be something funny or important.

Go to Twitter.com and signup for your free account.

Instagram – This is a photo sharing site. Post your photos to your followers and they will like it or repost it to their followers.

Go to Instagram.com to sign up for your free account.

LinkedIn - This is the business worlds' social media. You connect with others that you want to network with.

You can post articles, message other professionals all in one convenient site.

Go to Linkedin.com and signup for your free account.

Pinterest - This is a photo sharing site but you create your own board. A board is something meant to give you ideas within a certain specific parameter.

So if you are looking to remodel your office, you can pin photos of office décor that you like to give you ideas of how to do your remodel.

Go to Pinterest.com to sign up for your free account.

YouTube – This is a video website that allows you to find just about anything in the world.

It's awesome for "how to" or funny stupid human tricks. You can watch a rock concert from the 1970's or learn how to fix the leak in your sink.

You can create your own page and have subscribers who sign up for your videos. I would suggest creating videos for your business. It's a great way for prospects to get to know you.

Go to Youtube.com to sign up for your free account.

## Here's an example:

Harlan Kilstein is a great marketer. He owns this site called the Doggington Post. He has a website and a Facebook page.

The site is about dogs. They post on their Facebook page all things about dogs. Food, cute photos and videos, recalled items and animal cruelty.

Their mission is to celebrate dogs and their owners while pointing out to their fans those who abuse dogs.

It is a highly successful page on Facebook. It has a reach of about 750,000 people every week.

They make their money by selling items to their fans and by selling advertising. When you reach that many people, big companies want to show their products to a highly targeted audience.

## Call to Action:

Create your accounts today. Choose the ones that make sense to you and your business. Invite your current clients and your friends if appropriate.

Remember to have fun and be engaging!!

Start posting information. Do a bunch of posts all at once and have them scheduled to be released at about every 2 hrs. This keep you in front of people.

Try to have a system of something like; for every three good information posts you can make an offer to your followers.

Look into advertising for your business to gain followers. I'm using a generic term of "followers" so that it can apply to all of the above mentioned social media sites.

Social media is about engaging your followers. If you can't do this then this strategy may not be for you. But how can you not engage with someone who is being complimentary to you and your business.

That is what social media is mostly. All good. There are of course trolls or haters but ignore them. They hate their life and no one can fix that but them.

Besides, chances are they're jealous of you.

## Your Ideas

# STRATEGY #14

# HOST SEMINARS OR WORKSHOPS

Seminars or Workshops are a great way to get new clients. They can be as simple as having 6-10 people sitting in a room listening to your message or maybe a dinner at a restaurant with a message or a full blown all day or 3-day event with multiple speakers.

The purpose of these seminars/workshops is to educate your prospects and clients first and then offer them an opportunity to expand on this knowledge.

If people are willing to come to an event you are having; generally they are going to be your best clients/prospects to build your business on.

## Here's an Example:

I started my consulting business by doing a 90 minute workshop for potential clients. These potential clients were business owners, sales professionals, entrepreneurs and professional service providers.

It was a power point presentation that educated the attendees on the 3 ways to grow a business. It's why I wrote this learning tool.

I tried to concentrate on only a few of these strategies and not all of them. That would've been overload and most people would've left overwhelmed and that is not what I wanted.

At the end of the presentation, the attendees quite simply were able to leave or inquire to get more information on how I can help their particular businesses.

My goal going into the workshop was to get one good client. If people left and weren't interested in what I had to offer it wasn't a problem. Maybe we weren't a good fit. Keep in mind I will have their contact information so I can still send them quality information going forward.

At the end of the day; I was the expert in front of the room educating those in attendance. It is a vehicle to get in front of many in a short period of time. And it was building my brand.

This was a great technique to get clients and future clients in a non-threatening educational way.

## Call to Action:

First and foremost you need to decide what is best for your business immediately. Maybe a workshop will work best. Maybe a full blown seminar is ideal for you.

Here are some things you will need to figure out:

1) Date of event?

2) Location of event?

3) Physical location of event?

4) How long will the event be?

5) What will you teach or offer?

6) Will you charge for this?

7) How will you market this event?

8) How will you follow up after the event?

9) Will you offer anything for sale?

It's a lot of work but the rewards can be huge. I know people who are making 7-figures during a 3 day seminar. How much of that do you need to be happy?

## Your Ideas

# STRATEGY #15

## CREATE YOUR OWN NEWSLETTER

A newsletter is your marketing ace in the hole. Most companies do not offer newsletters and they are leaving a huge amount of money on the table.

Most businesses don't offer newsletters because they don't see the value of them. They see them as a time waster.

A newsletter is as simple as a one page information page of what is going on in your business. If you can make it at least two pages if not four; that will have the biggest impact.

Suggestions as to what to put into your newsletter is as simple as recipes, testimonials from clients, sales, new merchandise or funny stories. Really anything that would connect you and your client a little more than before you sent it out.

You can send these out to your clients as a hard copy newsletter or through an email to save costs. I suggest that you do it both ways.

It's important to have your clients address and email so that you can communicate with them more often and more effectively.

You can also sell a newsletter subscription that gives you very specific information on a niche that interests you. Most common is an investing or money making newsletter that offers information in a very compact package.

## Here's an example:

I'm a student of marketing guru Dan Kennedy. He sells a monthly marketing and business growth newsletter each month called the NO BS Marketing Newsletter.

His current rate is $59 per month and you get 16-20 pages of marketing tips and insights that will help any business. It is delivered to your home in a very loud envelope that you can't possible miss.

Dan has thousands of subscribers and he delivers content each month that is very desirable to his business clients.

He has taken the newsletter and put it on steroids. It is by far his biggest referral source and new client acquisition tool. He sells all of his seminars and products to his newsletter list and through the newsletter mailings.

This is a multi-million dollar newsletter that Dan created. He has worked hard at it and he deserves the fruits of his labor.

Some of the things you will find in his newsletter are client success stories and done-for-you marketing promotions that you can implement into your business immediately.

The genius of all of this is that most of the information he puts out is from his subscribers who send him their information with their results.

## Call to Action:

Search out other newsletters you subscribe to or find some to subscribe to. Look at what they are doing. Write down what you like and dislike.

Keep it simple in the beginning. The goal is to get it done and out in your clients and prospects hands.

Once you have the different subject categories figured out, all you have to do is write it. If you aren't a writer, look for guest writers or find writers on the internet that you can reprint in your newsletter.

This is easier than you think. Start it and see for yourself.

## Your Ideas

# STRATEGY #16

## DEVELOP YOUR UNIQUE SELLING PROPOSITION (USP)

A USP is your Unique Selling Proposition. It is meant to tell your prospect what it is you do in just a few words.

A perfect USP will be what your marketing surrounds itself with. It will take a brainstorming session to come up with yours but don't give up.

Please don't say that you're the best in customer service or that your products are the best. This is what every company will say. Your USP has to be client focused not focused on you.

If it can be enunciated as a benefit to your client or prospect, you will have the makings of a good USP.

It needs to be long enough to get your message told but not so long that it needs a minute to be read.

### Here's an example:

FedEx built their company around their USP *"When it absolutely, positively has to be there overnight... FedEx"*.

That USP told their clients and prospects that they will deliver their package anywhere overnight for them. It was perfect for the business that had super tight deadlines or a sale mattered on the information being delivered.

Keep in mind that computers were not what they are now so the timing for FedEx was perfect.

Another thing FedEx did was to guarantee their deliveries. This gave an assurance to the businesses that were sending their packages that this wasn't a joke. They were very serious.

This allowed FedEx to be the power house that they are today. They rocked it.

Dominoes Pizza had a USP that put them on the map also. Do you remember this one?

*"Fresh hot pizza in 30 minutes or less or its FREE !!"*

Dominoes was struggling before this USP. They were just another pizza place near a college campus. Nothing special.

This USP allowed Dominoes to open up locations all over the country and be an industry leader. They would've continued to struggle without these few little words put together in a sequence that resonated with the buying public.

## Call to Action:

I'm not going to lie to you. This is going to be a long tedious process to get it right.

Start by writing down all of things that make you  different than your competitors or the things that make your clients do business with you.

Remember this is not a tag-line. This is a mini mission statement that will distinguish your business as superior to your competitors and also at the same time tell your clients/prospects who you are and what you do.

It shouldn't be too long. It can start that way as you cipher it out.

I get a kick out of a flower shop I was working with that wanted to use several different USP's. This was very strategic because they advertise many different ways and that advertising reaches many different people and circumstances.

Here are a few we came up with:

-- *Flowers so beautiful, it will get you laid.*

-- *Flowers so beautiful, she will be putty in your hands.*

-- *Flowers so beautiful, she will forget why she is mad.*

-- *Flowers so beautiful, your friends will be jealous.*

-- *Flowers so beautiful, you will show how much you care.*

You can see why this is meant for some target markets and not others. They were not afraid to be confrontational.

Can you do something like this? Do you think it would work for you?

## Your Ideas

# STRATEGY #17

## USE DIRECT MAIL

Direct mail is considered a dinosaur by some marketers. Those marketers are fools. Direct mail is still a very effective means to get your message out to prospects and clients.

Direct mail is a letter, junk mail, a birthday card. It's something typically delivered by the Post Office but the other delivery companies are good too.

When direct mail is mentioned; it's typically thought of as a sales letter with an offer to purchase something or signup for something.

Direct mail has been the tool that great copywriters have used to get wealthy and companies have used to get rich. There is a famous saying in the marketing world that says "you are only one sales letter away from making more money then you could ever dream of."

Direct mail is just another tool in your tool box. It's a media. Which means it just one of the strategies you can use to get your message in the hands of clients/prospects. Nothing more and nothing less.

## Here's an example:

Gary Halbert was one of the pre-eminent copywriters in the world. He was responsible for mailing tens of millions of letters to households all over the U.S.

He sent out a sales letter called "The Coat of Arms" with your family's crest on it. He sold products with your crest on also. This campaign sold millions of dollars for several years. It was a huge success and all because of direct mail.

This was way before the internet existed so direct mail was one of the few ways to get your message out there. With everyone switching over to the internet, direct mail is a very viable alternative for your marketing.

## Call to Action:

You need to figure out what message you can send out and why you will send it.

Are you going for new clients? Are you sending this to existing clients? Are you sending this to prospects who haven't purchased yet?

Each of these groups need a different message.

Existing clients are the easiest because they like you already. This doesn't mean you should take them for granted it. You have to give them a reason to buy still. But you don't have to be on your "A" game to still get a response.

Prospects who haven't purchased yet at least know who you are and what you do. They may or may not remember you so you need to give them a reason why to do business with you. An irresistible offer is a great way to do this.

Getting New clients or using a mailing list is the hardest of the three groups of people. They haven't asked for anything from you before, they are being mailed to "cold".

The trick with them is to try to find something in common with you.

Consider this list:

1) Age

2) Wealth

3) Where they live

4) What they live in

5) Affinity group

6) Self interests

7) Race

8) Gender

9) Weight

10) Education

11) Hobbies

12) Family situation

13) Possessions

14) Profession

Now look at this list. Can you find your ideal client avatar from this list? Your avatar might contain several of these items.

My avatar for my putting green business was as follows:

-- *affluent white family with kids, college educated professional in a suburban sub division.*

Some of you will be offended by my avatar but after being in this business for 15 years, this applied to over 90% of my clients so why should I challenge my ideal prospect. I could literally go broke trying to change this avatar to a different avatar.

Getting back to your message, you want to start with a compelling benefit driven headline. Then a message that is educational and also letting them know that you have a solution to what they need.

At the end you want an irresistible offer that is a no brainer for them to make a decision. Finish with the different contact methods that will allow your prospect an easy way to respond.

Put this into an envelope that looks like personal mail. Please don't use a commercial looking envelope that will make it look like junk mail.

Good luck

## Your Ideas

# STRATEGY #18

## REVIVE OLD CLIENTS

Reviving old clients is the easiest way to get clients. They already have exposure with you. There are a few reasons why a client leaves. They could have moved away or no longer require your product or service. But the most heinous egregious way a client can leave you in the first place is by you ignoring them.

You probably think that each of your clients are sacred and you value each and every one of them. I'm not doubting that for a second. But here is where most businesses fail, hopefully not yours. During the sale you are spot on, you take care of their every whim. it's after the sale where businesses fail.

The lack of follow up is what drives a former client away. They forget about you. They move on to your competition. You don't give them a reason to come back.

You will need to create a follow up system that will allow you to touch your clients on a consistent basis. You can have a newsletter, or email offers to keep them engaged. Give them more information than offers however. You just can't only sell to them. You need to give them value.

## Here's an example:

The local dentist hopes their clients come for cleanings twice a year. They also hope that their clients schedule those cleanings at the time of their current cleaning. If they don't however, the likelihood of them coming back in six months is below 50%.

Dentists lose patients due to apathy all the time. Unfortunately the dentists have clients in front of them all the time so they don't realize when a patient leaves. It's too bad they don't have a follow up system in place so no one falls through the cracks.

One dentist put together a client retrieval system that offered their past clients a discounted cleaning with x-rays. It went out to everyone who hasn't been to the office in over one year. It was a great offer and it was very successful.

The dentist was able to revive 13% of their past clients. They mailed the same offer two more times and brought in another 15% of their past clients. 28% total. That's a huge boom for the dentists practice all because he took a few minutes to reach out to his old clients.

The key to the success of this campaign was to mail more than once. The trick to direct mail is to keep mailing to the list as long as it is profitable. One thing to mention with this particular mailing is that the dentist quit mailing after the third time only because he couldn't take any more patients.

## Call to Action:

Start by figuring out what you believe your sales cycle is. Some businesses it could be 30 days, others 6 months and still others 1 year.

If a client passes your time threshold, they can be considered lost clients. Meaning they may have moved on to some other business, no longer need your business, moved away, etc.

This won't happen to you after reading this book because you will be in constant communication with all of your clients from now on... right????

But right now, you probably haven't been staying in touch so let us get back in touch with your clients.

Create an irresistible offer to get them back. We have mentioned this a lot in this book so I think you have an idea by now of what to offer and how to offer it.

## Your Ideas

# STRATEGY #19

## LEVERAGE QUALIFIED CLIENT AND PROSPECT LISTS

Client lists and mailing lists can make your business a lot of money. Hopefully you have developed your own prospect and client lists. If not start today.

Mailing lists are lists of names of people who fall into different categories. This is very helpful if you are going to launch a marketing campaign.

It's quite easy to start your own list. You can ask the people who come into your store. You can get the email list of your visitors to your website or blog. There are countless ways to do this. Some even run ads to just get names to create a prospect list.

The purpose of your own list is to market to them with offers for them to purchase. It also is to educate them on your products or services to get closer to making a buying decision.

Renting mailing lists is an option also. You can create a very targeted group of people by doing this. If you need divorced mothers with children, they have it available to you.

The trick with mailing lists is to try to find something in common with your clients.

Consider this list:

1) Age

2) Wealth

3) Where they live

4) What they live in

5) Affinity group

6) Self interests

7) Race

8) Gender

9) Weight

10) Education

11) Hobbies

12) Family situation

13) Possessions

14) Profession

Now look at this list. Can you find your ideal client avatar from this list? Your avatar might contain several of these items.

My avatar for my putting green business was as follows:

-- *affluent white family with kids, college educated professional in a suburban sub division.*

anything else you may be able to think of.

The purpose of renting a list is to do a campaign and build your client list. You can use this list along with a direct mail campaign to target your ideal client.

## Here's an example:

I have rented mailing list from a couple of different companies. These lists are rented and not owned because you don't own the original list that these names comes from. Someone else does so you need to respect the owners of the names wishes. They are loan to you for one mailing unless you ask for more mailings to the list.

I mentioned earlier that I did a postcard mailing for my putting green business. I selected golfers with children who have an average income of $100,000 and a home valued at $350,000. I chose the list of names for my area and for the Chicago market. That's a fairly targeted list.

I wanted those dynamics because over the years I have been able to create an Avatar of who my ideal client is.

There were about 2000 names that met the criteria I set forth. I sent out the postcard received 5 leads and one sale. I never would have made that sale without using a rented mailing list.

## Call to Action:

Remember back to direct mail and the call to action for that strategy?

Well it isn't any different for this one.

Create your ideal client or avatar. Find a list broker and let them know what you are looking for. They will match up your avatar down to exact detail you want to use. Keep in mind the more "selects" you use the more expensive your rented list will be. A "select" is the different parameters you give them to narrow down your avatar.

If you haven't figured out your ideal client or avatar yet then go through your client list and take notes. Hopefully you know who your clients are and can create an avatar from memory.

If you don't know, you can send out a survey for your clients to fill in the blanks. Ask for their help. A good portion will help you. Offer some type of incentive for them if they help you.

This will help you in more ways than you will ever know and it can be accomplished in a day.

## Your Ideas

# STRATEGY #20

## LEVERAGE EMAILS OFFERS AND EDUCATION

In today's world the internet has made some things easier to market to your clients. It definitely has made contacting your prospects and clients much more efficient.

Emailing is the most used way a business communicates with their clients. It's easy and more importantly it's FREE.

Email should be done two ways:

1st- it should be used to send out information to educate your clients. Educate them with knowledge of the products, the industry you are in or any other piece of information that your clients would be interested in.

2nd- It's ok to send out an offer to purchase something as long as you have been giving value along the way. An offer once or twice a week will not offend anyone. If it does… too bad for them.

### Here's an example:

Ryan Deiss has spent thousands and thousands of dollars testing what the best formula there is for sending out emails.

He has figured that sending out five emails a week is optimal and that there should be three emails that offer great value to your list and two days that offer products or services for sale.

He is in the internet marketing niche so he sells and also gives away information. He has made millions using this formula and I think it's a good one to model.

Do you have 5 days worth of emails to send out each week? Do you think that is overkill? You have to find your sweet spot with your list. Chances are you can send out more information and they won't mind as long as you give value.

## Call to Action:

You will need to find out how much information you can send your list. Is your business full of information or is it so niche that it's up to you to do the creating.

If it's a big niche like internet marketing or golf, you will have thousands of examples available to you that you can use to educate your list.

Unfortunately you will not know how often you should contact them until you do and see the results for yourself. This falls under "testing". Some of you can email twice per day and be good. Some will only be able to email once a week.

You can tell by the number of unsubscribes that you get. It's important to be in tuned with what your list will except from you. Just getting an unsubscribe isn't necessarily a bad thing. Sometimes those who truly aren't interested will simply fall off. You have to gauge this by your gut feeling or stats. Whichever you're more comfortable with.

Remember the Golden Rule that Ryan Deiss has set up. More education than offers. Give value before taking their money.

## Your Ideas

# STRATEGY #21

## HOST A WEBINAR

Webinars are power point presentations that are internet based. These have grown at an unbelievable rate over the years. I remember when the top marketers were all doing these and having no success at all with these. Now they are super successful.

You can do these live or pre-recorded depending on how you want to use them.

I assumed that you know what a power point presentation is but just as a refresher, it's a group of slides that are either text, photos, music, recorded voice or video. Of course it can be a combination of these also.

It's meant to be a sales presentation that would lead a prospect along the buying cycle with an end goal of making a sale or to get more information.

You have to sign up to attend a webinar so it is also a way to start an email list.

### Here's an example:

I recently watched a webinar from Preston Ely a real estate investor who was selling his software program to find and sell deals.

It was 18min. long and walked you through his sales pitch on this software. It was not only informative but very well done. It incorporated an illustrator who illustrates different situations that Preston brings up during his webinar.

What Preston did differently with his webinar is that it wasn't something you signed up for. It was something that played when you landed on his site. It was a lead generation tool and it was masterful.

Preston has signed up thousands of investors to use his software as a result of this webinar. Not a bad way to make millions of dollars.

The best part of it is that it's evergreen which means you do it once and you can use it over and over.

## Call to Action:

First of all you need a message to deliver. This is also meant for a regional or national selling situation but I know that it could be done locally.

Webinars are big business now. It really is nothing more than a power point presentation that keeps on playing in an evergreen format.

So besides the text and graphics, there can be video, music and also the ability to live draw or write on a slide.

You also want to consider it as a sales presentation for your product or service so keep that in mind when you craft your presentation.

This is a good rule of thumb for you to follow:

1) Welcome them
2) Tell them what you're going to tell them
3) Introduce yourself
4) Tell them why they should listen to you
5) Tell them the information
6) Engage with them along the way by asking questions
7) Make your offer
8) Make it easy for them to order

## Your Ideas

# STRATEGY #22

# WRITE A BOOK

I always wanted to be an author. I wrote this learning tool so that I can say "I'm an author" and to cross it off my bucket list.

I also wrote this book to grow my business. Authors are considered experts plain and simple. It doesn't even matter if they're dumb as a bag of rocks. I'm not by the way.

This book will open doors for me that might have been closed before. It will be my business card of sorts. In fact it will be the best business card I'll ever have.

Writing a book is about discipline and having something to say that allows people to think of you as an expert. Being an expert gives you an edge up on your competition.

Writing a book is important. It will give you credibility. You will be more credible to your clients, your peers, your prospects and to the media. It will help tremendously with PR. Remember that from earlier?

## Here's an example:

Dan Kennedy has written a couple of dozen books. He doesn't write them to make money off of the books through book sales. He does however write them to make money.

He taught me years ago that writing books is good to get high paying consulting jobs. That's it... nothing else. The sales from the books themselves won't add up to much. Sorry you're not Stephen King or John Grisham.

He says he has made millions of dollars from his books but in the non-traditional way. Like a very smart marketer, he knew this all along. That's why he is one of the very best.

## Call to Action:

Obviously you will need a topic to write about. I truly believe everyone has at least one book in them. It doesn't matter if the subject has been covered before. You will most likely bring a different perspective to the subject matter.

A friend of mine gave me his method to writing and you can find a lot of ways to write on the internet with a simple search.

His method was to write an outline of the different topics you want to cover. Each topic is a chapter or a sub-chapter of a bigger topic you will write about.

He then told me to write a paragraph on each topic and voila you are 90% done. You may want to include graphics, you'll need a title for the book, you'll probably want an ISBN#, etc.

If you're not a writer, you can speak into a recorder and then transcribe it later. This is a very quick and easy way to write.

Lastly you can have someone write the book for you. It's costly but it will get done.

## Your Ideas

# STRATEGY #23

## EXHIBIT AT TRADESHOWS

Many companies exhibit at their trade association's annual showcase. These tradeshows are a way for companies to show off their products and services to others in the industry.

There are buyers that come to these shows that wouldn't normally be available to these companies. It's also a great place to showcase the brand new merchandise that no one has seen before.

Along with buyers, there are also media from the industry trade magazines and other sources that can make the shows worthwhile to attend.

Buyers and the media are good reasons to go but you better have a plan. A plan to get as many leads as you can to follow up with. The show is not necessarily for selling although that could happen.

There are numerous ways to get leads at the show. You can have a raffle, you can do a contest of some type, you can be a sponsor where you get the names of the attendees, you can even have scantily clad ladies to bring the men in, etc. etc.

Whatever you do, do it with vigor and then follow-up with them.

## Here's an example:

Chet Holmes was one of my favorite sales mentors. He tells a story of when he would run a tradeshow booth. At the time he ran seven different magazines for a billionaire named Charlie Mungher.

Being in the magazine business meant you sold advertising. That meant you wined and dined clients to secure business.

At tradeshows, Chet would schedule appointments all day with clients. He knew the show would be good to get all of the heavy hitters in one area in a very tight window. Perfect for Chet who was a selling machine and who had to make the most out of being at the show as an exhibiter.

Chet also knew that most people coming to these shows were from out of town. So he would pre-book a number of reservations at the hottest night club in town. He would let them drink for free and make sure they were treated like royalty.

Every year Chet and his parties were the talk of the show and it inevitably made him the most sought out person and booth at the show because you had to see Chet to get a pass for the club.

What no one knew is that Chet called around to the best clubs and asked the manager for a deal. He told the manager that he wanted to bring 100 VIP clients to their club and he wanted to pay the bill which meant to the manager an open bar. Cha-ching.

The manager always gave Chet a good price on drinks and also kicked in for some food and also everyone got in for FREE. No cover and immediate access like Paris Hilton gets. He was able to give a 1st class party for not much money.

There is a right way to do tradeshows and a wrong way. Which way do you do it?

## Call to Action:

Every part of your booth space should be considered. It's very expensive real estate. Use every inch of it to get your prospects attention.

You need to have a concise goal of what you want to accomplish at your tradeshows. Make a list and the best way to go about accomplishing each goal.

1) Get leads

2) Meet industry heavy weights

3) Client meetings

4) Educate prospects

5) Speak in breakout sessions

6) Have fun

7) Throw a party

8) Be the expert

## Your Ideas

# STRATEGY #24

## START PUBLIC SPEAKING

Public speaking scares the crap out of people. The notion of having eyes on them watching every move is too much for some.

It is also one of the highest paid professions you can get into. You don't have to become a professional to experience the power of speaking.

Speaking on a local level is an extremely strategic way to get new clients into your business. Those in the audience will automatically see you as an expert because you were thought of enough to be there speaking.

You can speak at a corporate function or a local chamber of commerce meeting. Somewhere where people gather to learn. Learn whatever it is you have to talk about. It's very powerful.

There is also the local media for you to speak for. They are always looking for stories or fill to take up time on their radio or TV shows.

### Here's an example:

There's a local chef where I live who has grown his restaurant business by being on TV during the morning shows.

He is a very charismatic man and as he demonstrates how he prepares a dish, he is also funny. It plays well on camera and it has played well at his restaurant. He has opened two different locations since he started using this strategy.

The public sees him as a celebrity chef because he is on TV. Public speaking has built his business. Oh... and the food is awesome.

## Call to Action:

Business groups, chambers of commerce, civic clubs, and countless other groups need speakers to make their events more attractive to attendees.

Create a speech on a topic that will appeal to the group you are talking to. Public speaking is terrifying to a lot of people so speakers are in need.

Follow the outline I gave you for developing a webinar. I'll repost it below changing it a little.

1) Welcome them

2) Tell them what you're going to tell them

3) Introduce yourself

4) Tell them why they should listen to you

5) Tell them the information

6) Engage with them along the way by asking questions

7) Let them get more information about you and your business

## Your Ideas

# STRATEGY #25

# WRITE A BLOG

Blogs have become very mainstream over the last few years. A blog is similar to an online diary. It's as simple as writing a few lines of text similar to posting an update on Facebook.

That is the very basic way of using a blog. A much more sophisticated way to have a blog is the Huffington Post. Looks like a website right? It's not. It's a very successful and highly visible blog.

Blogs are also SEO'd at a very quick rate. It is usually highly relevant content and because of that fact, Google indexes the information fast.

You can use blogs to post funny stories, how-to information, client testimonials, videos, photos or whatever your mind can think of.

Blogs are extremely versatile and easily designed with various plug-ins that are available to add that website look to your blog.

## Here's an example:

Arianna Huffington started the Huffington Post back in 2005. Not that long ago. She sold it for $315 million in 2011.

Not a bad pay day for a few years work. Now keep in mind that there was a tremendous amount of work that went into that blog. Dozens of posts per day, consumer engagement, ad revenue, etc.

My point is that this blog started as an idea and became one of the country's most trusted blog sites.

Is it possible that you can create a blog that has influence over your clients, prospects and possible future leads? I know that you can.

## Call to Action:

This is a chance to get your ideas out to the world or at least to your clients and prospects.

Blogs are typically set up like Microsoft Word. You type your thoughts and you can pick fonts, etc.

Start by having a plan. Keep each thought you have to write about as a separate blog post. That way you can be precise about your thoughts and the ideas you want to share.

If you aren't a writer, write anyway. I promise you will find your "voice" eventually and when you do it will be magic.

I was able to set up a blog fairly easily using "Tumblr" but there are others like "Blogger" to use also. If you want your blog to be designed like say the Huffington Post, you will need a web designer to do that for you if you don't know how to.

## Your Ideas

# STRATEGY #26

# WRITE ARTICLES

In the same vein as writing a blog, writing an article is also effective. Articles can be written for your newsletter, or someone else's newsletter. They can be written for a strategic alliance who wants to give value to their clients. The sky's the limit.

Articles are another way to be viewed as an expert. Just like other strategies mentioned, becoming a celebrity is valuable to you.

Don't worry about the amount of words or the size of the font. If you are writing for a publication, they will have a criteria sheet for you to review so that you can submit everything according to their wishes.

You can also write for article listing sites. These sites host your articles and other publications will find your article there and post it to their site. It could be a blog or email. Whatever would fit their needs at the time.

Keep in mind that writing is just putting your thoughts down on paper. No sweat.

## Here's an example:

Consultants especially marketing consultants will look for clients in any niche they can. A smart consultant will have an article on "marketing 101" already in the can ready to go at a moment's notice.

They will take that article and submit it to every relevant niche they can find. I'll give you a couple of examples.

A magazine/catalogue who sells high end music equipment that only performers would buy from might need information on how to market their band better to get good gigs.

A photographer who loves to take photos of nature is reading a photography tips magazine. She always wanted to sell her photos and this article in her magazine will help her start.

Easy isn't it? There's a need for great relevant content. You could be in several different publications all at once.

Brainstorm for a few minutes on who would want or need your articles. Start submitting them.

## Call to Action:

Have you noticed there are a lot of writing strategies listed in this book? That's not your imagination.

Writing is one of the quickest ways to be considered an expert or an authority on a subject matter. This is why writing is very important. Plus they all blend well together.

A blog post can be an article. An article can be a blog post. Both can be packaged up and put into a book. Both can also be sent as an educational email. You see one thing can be four things or more.

So just like writing a blog post, start with a list of topics you have knowledge on and write.

Try submitting these articles to your local paper or websites like "Reddit" or any other site in your niche. And don't forget about newsletters. They can be a very powerful way to get your message out.

## Your Ideas

# STRATEGY #27

## INCREASE THE SALES SKILLS OF YOUR STAFF

You may believe that only your sales staff is in sales. This is a very common belief. The truth is that everyone in your company is in sales whether they want to be or not.

In a traditional company setting you probably have someone who answers the phone when it rings. That person is the first impression of your company that the caller receives.

If your receptionist answers any way that they feel like, it will give a negative impression to anyone who calls. The reverse obviously is true also.

If you are a retailer and the cashier or stock clerk isn't familiar with your product lines and isn't knowledgeable on what or why you carry a certain line of products; what does that say to your client?

Obviously if your employees are part time help from high school or college, you are happy if they just show up. That needs to stop and stop now.

Knowing that they are not experts like you are on the products and services you offer is a good first step in the process. Start by hiring staff who has an interest or background in your products or services.

Teaching your staff will take a long time. In today's world, training an employee is a dying art form. You want to train them on a section at a time so you don't overwhelm them.

OK. Training isn't sales but first things first. Your staff needs a basic understanding of what the benefits your products or services provide before they can help sell for you.

Teach your staff very limited but certain suggestive sells. Cross sells and up sells are the easiest way your staff can help you.

Cross sells are products that compliment what it is that you're selling. Up sells are selling more expensive items of the same product or maybe a larger quantity of the same product.

These two strategies alone will boost your sales tremendously. It's something that will make sense to your staff as well.

## Here's an example:

McDonald's wasn't the first company to implement sales strategies into their staff but it is the first one that I can remember.

Most agree that McDonald's doesn't offer the best food or have the most talented employees. No offense to the employees but they are mostly there to learn skills to move on to bigger and better opportunities. Like everyone else.

What McDonald's has done is to create Up sells and Cross sells for their employees to sell their menu items. And they do it without fail in any location you go into or drive thru.

An example of McDonald's using a cross sell comes very naturally even to a 16yr old kid behind the counter. They are taught sayings based on what the guest orders. The famous line "would you like fries with that?" is a cross sell. "Would you like a soda with your order" is also a cross sell.

These cross sells are professionally executed by staff who never had formal training and they are making millions of dollars each year by doing something this simple.

An up sell for McDonald's has gotten them into some trouble with those fighting obesity. Have you ever been asked "would you like to Supersize that meal?"

There was even a documentary about this phenomenon called "Supersize Me". They had to promise to stop asking their guests if they wanted to "Supersize that" because it worked too good.

Another up sell that McDonald's does is to offer the "meal Deal". It's a higher ring total but it simplifies the ordering process for the staff member and the guest. Another multi-million dollar sales strategy.

You see, you don't have to complicate things. Just give your staff some basic tools that will have a powerful impact for you on the balance sheet.

## Call to Action:

Company training has become an expense to businesses. It's a shame really. Maybe companies have grown tired of training an employee especially a part-time employee and having them quit a few weeks later. Every business owner has had this happen to them.

I want you to keep this in mind; your employees are usually the first people that your clients and prospects interact with.

As I mentioned earlier, start with small bites. Give your employees one thing they can sell or one concept that will help them in several areas.

Teaching them up-sells and cross-sells alone will increase your bottom line tremendously and shouldn't be too hard to train your staff on.

Most of the time you will need to create these for them. Better yet, if your staff has a good understanding of what it is that you want to accomplish they can help you create them.

If they are involved in the decision making process, they will take ownership of the process and make it their own. That's a Win-Win !!

# Your Ideas

# STRATEGY #28

## EDUCATE YOUR CLIENTS

A smarter better educated client is someone who will trust you and spend more money with you.

Every client has different needs from one another. They are typically at different levels of aptitude. Let's look at your clients as either beginner, intermediate, advanced and expert.

Each skill or knowledge level requires different needs. The beginner needs different information or training that the advanced client needs. I think you get this.

Educating your clients keeps them engaged with you because they will seek you out especially if they are passionate about what you have to offer.

The beginner will take the most time and effort because they don't know yet if they are interested in you or your product or service. They are trying to figure this out.

As an incentive to you to train and educate beginners is the fact that they will purchase a tremendous amount of goods to figure out if they want to proceed with what it is you offer.

And as your clients ascend the ladder of aptitude and knowledge, there will be more products and services they will need to accomplish their new goals.

## Here's an example:

Wine shops are a classic example of businesses who educate their clients. The good ones anyway. Wine is a niche that has so much information and knowledge to learn as well as wine to taste.

My wife and I had a favorite wine bar by our house. We went there the first time not knowing much about wine at all but knew it was a quality night out at the very least.

We started wine as White Zinfandel drinkers. Most do because it is a sweeter wine and it isn't complex. Wine drinkers have to train their palettes for different flavor profiles that wine offers. Something we had to learn.

The owners knew how to cultivate a client. They weren't experts themselves but they knew how to ascend their clients through a process that taught about wine.

They brought in experts and wine makers for special events where these industry insiders taught their clients. Did you catch the fact that the owners weren't experts but they were smart enough to bring them in?

What happened over time was a more educated consumer. A consumer that as they get educated will buy more wine because they want to try as many varietals as they can.

A varietal is the grape that wine is made from. There are special and unique grapes to almost all wine. You've heard of Merlot and Shiraz right? Well they are different grapes grown in different climates and altitudes.

This is why education is so important. Any wine bar can pour a cab for you but the successful one will educate you also and offer you the opportunity to learn as much as you want to about wine.

Our wine bar offered a wine club with tasting notes and recipes to further your knowledge and enjoyment of wine. They offered wine flights so you could have smaller tastes of a particular wine but have more variety so you could further your knowledge.

Wine is an industry where you will never really know everything. That is why it is fascinating to my wife and I. Because we have educated ourselves, we have been on many winery tours including Washington state, California and Rioja in Spain.

That's a big leap from where we started with White Zinfandel and have gladly spent thousands of dollars learning all of the way.

## Call to Action:

No doubt about it an educated consumer is a better consumer. This transcends any industry.

An educated consumer also tends to buy more things. They will gravitate to that source of education more times than not.

What does that mean? It means that if you do the educating they will reward you for it by patronizing your business.

Start by doing your emails like we discussed earlier. Have signage in your store that also give a tip or knowledge on your product.

Do videos on your website especially if it is a how-to type of presentation. Hire staff that are passionate about the subject matter of your business so that they can be ambassadors and educators for you.

Offer books and other material that furthers the education of your clients.

Remember they look to you as the experts in this particular field. They want to be guided.

An uneducated prospect will be a bad client. It's just the way the world works.

## Your Ideas

# STRATEGY #29

## CREATE SPECIAL EVENTS

Special events are a way to get your clients excited for something. They could be centered around a big sale or live music. Pretty much whatever your brain comes up with.

Most businesses do special events once a year on their anniversary date. Others on the other hand are very creative and try to do one every day of the week. Have you ever heard of the special days calendar?

It's a calendar for the "National day of _____". You've heard of these. Today as I write this its "national rubber ducky day". How cute.

Be creative. Your clients will love it and respond. You'll be surprised at what they will like and not like.

### Here's an example:

There were three small retailers by my house that all started in business in different years but at the same time of year (November).

They all decided to have one big anniversary sale together.

It made sense because they were each going to have them anyway so they figured why not. They created a marketing piece that featured each of the businesses and how many years it was they were celebrating.

Each of their clients list received the same marketing piece. It was an oversized post card that they shared together as one.

Each business ran their separate event though. They were no longer together during the Anniversary weekend they planned as a group of three. They had Power in numbers going for them and they let it slip away.

What do I mean in the last paragraph? Well, I'll go through a Good vs. Bad list because it could've been special but instead was just okay.

## Good:

They came together and pooled their clients lists to get a lot of people to come to their event. This was good because it now gave a shopper more of a reason to swing in because it was now three stores who had special offerings. Power in numbers.

They also offered raffle prizes to those who stopped by and filled out a slip. This built their client lists even more because most of their current clients who stopped by brought a friend. No one likes to shop alone type of mentality.

They had discounts on select merchandise that shoppers could only take advantage of during the Anniversary weekend which gave their clients a sense of urgency.

There was an offering of appetizers and festive drinks for shoppers to make it even more special. They did a lot of things right.

## Bad:

They made a couple of critical errors however and maybe this is just the consultant in me looking for ways to improve on something.

During the weekend, the businesses were no longer a threesome working together. They were individual businesses that acted independently from one another.

They didn't take the power of three different mailing lists and create a larger spaced event. I mentioned earlier that it was November so doing anything outside is dicey at best but a heated tent with music would've worked and the heat from the bodies that would be in there also would've made this work.

There was no follow up from any of the three businesses to their clients showing how much fun everyone was having.

This would've accomplished two things:

First it would've showed the clients who missed out that they probably should've been there.

Second it allows those that came a chance to hear about the winners of the raffles and maybe seeing themselves in a photo from one of the businesses while they were shopping or taking in the refreshments.

Hindsight is 20/20 and as a consultant it's very easy to be a back seat driver but a great consultant can offer a set of fresh eyes to something and make it better. It goes back to an old saying "you can't see the forest through the trees".

## Call to Action:

Go online and check out any number of special day calendars. This will give you tons of inspiration and create some ideas.

It can also really fill in your marketing calendar. A marketing calendar is a calendar that lists all of your marketing tasks, roll-outs, campaigns and events. It's not an hourly schedule like a planner, it's a giant overview of your plan.

Plan for an event or a special day that you can embrace easily. It will be easier to pull off if it's fun.

Please pick something that you think your clients will respond to.

## Your Ideas

# STRATEGY #30

## CONDUCT INTERVIEWS

Getting yourself interviewed makes you look like an expert. Only experts get interviewed. That is what the public thinks.

There are many reasons to get interviewed. It could be part of a PR campaign and you were soliciting to be interviewed on a certain topic. You could have special knowledge that was needed to do a news story about a trending topic. Or you could have a friend interview you as a way to create a marketing piece for your clients.

My advice is to be interviewed as often as you can and in as many different medias as you can. Radio, TV, Print, CD/DVD all have tremendous upside to you.

Another way to do this strategy is to interview experts in your field and the field of your clients.

There are experts everywhere who will want to share their expertise with you.

### Here's an example:

The easiest place to start is by creating your own CD to give away to your prospects or clients as a marketing tool to help you and your business.

I created several of these CD's over the years on many different topics. They are easy to make and very powerful to use. It further solidified me as an expert to my clients. I know I have mentioned expert status a lot here but it's that important. It will help in ways you will never realize until you start embracing the fact.

There's a free service out there called Freeconferencccall.com They will give you a call in phone number with a pass code so you can hold a conference call if you'd like.

I use it to record my phone calls or in this case, to record my interviews. They will also give me the mp3 recording of the call. You can have multiple people on one call.

The mp3 can simply be downloaded and burned onto a disk to hand out or sell. Whatever it is your trying to accomplish. The mp3 can also be edited and have intro music put on it or whatever you may need. It really is as simple as I stated.

## Call to Action:

Does this open up some ideas in your brain? Start making a list of topics that you can talk or discuss immediately. Remember, if you know more about a topic than someone who would receive this CD, then you are an expert and you can speak intelligently on the subject you have chosen.

Contact local and regional radio, newspaper and TV stations and send them a press release.

Web based radio stations are really popping up a lot now and need experts to interview.

Start making contacts. It may not pay off immediately but it will pay off.

Also make a list of experts you want to interview. This should be easy for you. Just make sure your clients will want to listen to what they have to say. This may be a good way to start if you are uncomfortable being the center of attention. You will become very comfortable interviewing experts because they have the pressure, you have the questions.

## Your Ideas

# STRATEGY #31

## LEVERAGE PAY PER CLICK (PPC)

Pay per click are ads placed on Google either on top, bottom or side of the page. The ads include a headline and a brief description all based upon what it was you were searching for on Google.

The companies listed on Google pay only when someone clicks on their ad. The price that they pay depends on how many competitors there are and how much a company is willing to pay.

When you click on the ad you will be taken to the company's website you clicked on. It's a very effective and quick way to start a mailing list or test an idea you have to see if it has merit.

### Here's an example:

Perry Marshall is an authority on the subject of Pay per click advertising. He has taught thousands of people and has made millions of dollars using (PPC) advertising.

He creates campaigns for anything from book sales, seminars, webinars, newsletters, etc.

He will test about 100 different headlines and descriptions to see what performs the best. He only gets rid of those campaigns that don't make money.

If you're wondering why he doesn't only keep the best campaign; it's because people will use different search phrases or key words. Everyone's brain is different. Plus if it makes money it's a winner.

It might be the quickest way to get a client ever invented. Not everyone does it because you have to pay money to do it so that knocks a lot of people out of the game before they even start.

## Call to Action:

Contact Google and apply to start an account. They will review your website to see if it meets their criteria. They do this because they want real companies with real products and information who are also reputable.

Create your ad. It will contain a benefit based headline with a description of why they should go to your site.

It's vitally important to have a daily budget in mind for your campaign. Google will not go over your daily budget. They are respectful of it. You also need to have a plan in place for why you are spending this money.

Please don't spend to spend. This is just like any other business decision.

Lastly have an overall plan for your website or blog that you send this traffic to. This will be a very expensive experiment if you don't do this correctly.

## Your Ideas

# STRATEGY #32

# NETWORK WITH OTHERS

Who hasn't been to an after work meet and greet to pick up someone or to get a few business cards. Those are awful.

I'm not telling you to not do them because there is business to be had at those. It's just a painful process.

I like the ones that are part of business meetings. These lend themselves to a more professional crowd.

Networking can also be done on a one-to-one basis like over a cup of coffee or a quick bite to eat. This will be your best networking opportunities.

Networking allows for you to meet a lot of people quickly. Also a lot of people who can help your business.

Please just don't collect business cards and throw them in a draw.

## Here's an Example:

My good friend Kevin Kowalke is the Grand Pulbah of a group called the Thursday Morning Thing. 100 business owners and sales professionals come together once a month to learn a new business strategy to implement in their business.

Before and after the meeting there is a time to network with other serious professionals that are truly interested in growing their businesses. It is literally a room full of gold nuggets.

Kevin has painstakingly weeded out anyone who doesn't follow his vision for the group. It's a big reason it's the best place in Milwaukee to learn and network.

## Call to Action:

Do yourself a favor and find a group like mine to network in. It will be money and time well spent.

Look for your local chambers of commerce, Better Business Bureau, Association, etc. Any group that has groups of businesses is a good place to start.

Now when you approach people, please don't tell them how great you are. Ask them what they need help with or talk with them to see if you would be a good fit for you.

It's your job to see if you can help them because they are only thinking of themselves.

Find out how you can benefit them and ease their pains. Whatever they may be.

## Your Ideas

# STRATEGY #33

## START TELEMARKETING

Are you saying to yourself telemarketing? Isn't that illegal and why would I do that?

Telemarketing isn't illegal but there is a "No Call" list that every state has and you will need to follow that. Non-profits and politicians get around the "no call" list though.

The telemarketing I'm suggesting however is for those prospects and clients who have given you permission to contact them by phone. You will need to be sensitive to those that want to be removed from further contact by phone however.

You can use a service to do this for you or you can do it yourself. That is up to you. It will depend upon your message.

Pre-recorded messages meant to only play on an answering machine is also a great option for this strategy. You may be receiving these type of messages on your cell phones now. Powerful stuff.

Believe me, telemarketing is still a valuable tool if used correctly. And another thing, you will need to have this scripted. I'll explain that in a little bit.

## Here's an example:

Ron LeGrand is a real estate investor out of Tampa Bay, FL. He is also the nation's premiere teacher in regards to real estate investing.

Ron's number one tool for getting new clients is telemarketing.

What he does is he has several different lead generation methods that bring in prospects. He has radio ads, TV ads, Facebook ads, print ads, etc. You name it, Ron has done it.

All of these ads lead to either an answering machine or a live person who collects the prospects information that he promptly sends out a CD or DVD based on what ad they responded to. Ron is always testing this. Sounds familiar doesn't it?

Ron then has a telemarketing firm in place to make follow-up calls to these prospects. They ask if they received the information and want to learn more about investing. They then sell the prospects on a live event he has to further their knowledge.

Ron is approaching Billionaire status so I know this works and he couldn't think of doing his business without telemarketing.

The telemarketing firm just follows a script that Ron has tested over the years and they just replicate his words and him ion each call.

## Call to Action:

First things first, you need to develop a plan on why you would want to incorporate telemarketing into your business. Just like any other strategy in this book.

Develop a sales script for your staff, telemarketing company and you to follow along with. The script will need to follow a flow of a regular conversation.

It will need to have a list of responses ready for any objection you may encounter along the way. It will also need to have a path for when you come across a buyer.

Once you have a rough draft of a script, test it out on a friend or family member to work out any kinks.

Try to keep this script short enough to keep the attention of your client or prospect but not too long where they hang up on you.

You will want to test different length scripts to see where your best results will come from.

Pre-recorded messages will be no different. Shorter is typically better but it needs to tell your information.

One last thing, your message must contain only one idea or call to action. Do not put in five different sales pitches promoting five different things. One call, one promotion or idea.

## Your Ideas

# STRATEGY #34

## SHOWCASE YOURSELF ON TV OR RADIO

There's nothing that says expert or celebrity than being on your local TV and radio stations. If you can make it on regional or national shows, that's even better.

Show producers are always looking for stories. Feel good, exposé stuff and anything else that the public will find interesting.

It's a lot of work with potentially huge payoffs. You will also be able to brand yourself afterwards by using the radio spot or TV spot in your marketing to your clients and prospects.

It will come down to "look at me, I'm an expert. You should listen to me and support my business because of this". Obviously that is something you do not enunciate, you keep it to yourself. I'm just saying that it will have that effect on you so don't let it get to your head.

Pompous asses are not my intention.

### Here's an Example:

Restaurant chefs have long since used TV to get themselves and their restaurants some FREE publicity.

Cooking works so well on TV because it is very visual. It also works well because it seems like the hosts never cook or are just learning so they ask basic questions that can help everyone.

The recipes are always easy enough that anyone can feel they can manage it and it always looks so damn good that I want to eat the TV screen.

The key to the whole show is to give away the recipe because who doesn't want another recipe? If the chef was also selling a cookbook that would be even better.

On the recipe it has the chefs contact information and if they are smart it also offers a coupon to come into their restaurant especially if this is a local show.

## Call to Action:

Start by contacting your local radio and TV show producers. It's common for people to produce multiple shows so you aren't contacting a whole bunch of people.

Keep in mind the shows target audience. If you have something that would be great for senior citizens, don't contact a radio station who has a young audience base. It isn't a good fit.

Start with a concise message. Something like "the 3 ways to stretch your social security checks out longer". People like lists so if you can come up with the 3 or 5 or 7 best ways of doing something; it will help you tremendously.

Treat this as a Press Release. Remember that from earlier in the book?

All of this blends together doesn't it?

## Your Ideas

# STRATEGY #35

## CREATE A CD OR DVD

This isn't as hard as you think. We are not talking about going into a record studio like musicians and spending thousands of dollars on creating a master piece.

There's a website you can go to and record yourself or record an interview with someone else or a group of people. It's called Freeconferencecall.com

It's very easy to use and they will record it for you. You can then burn the recording to a CD and slap a label on it.

Simple right?

DVD's aren't that difficult either. You can record on most cell phones now and the quality is pretty good. You can also buy a HD camera inexpensively now so you have options.

Same idea as a CD. You burn it to DVD when you are done.

Editing software will clean up anything you don't like so that isn't a problem either and if you dread the idea of editing your work, you can hire it out to someone that can incorporate sound and text where appropriate.

The business strategy as to why you do this is quite simple. You are giving up a piece of you to give your clients and prospects more information, more of you, more of your business.

This is done to further your relationship together. Hopefully it's what you want for your business and yourself.

You can charge money for this information or you can give it away FREE. Whatever you want to do with it.

If you give it away for FREE make sure you have a plan in place and that you have a good reason to do so.

## Here's an example:

I have created several CD's in my life. They were very simple to do and it didn't seem overwhelming to me. Electronics and technology have a love/hate relationship with me and I'm OK with that.

I started out with a strategic plan in mind. I created a giveaway CD that explained to my prospects who I was and what I helped businesses with.

I gave example strategies and how it can help their business if they were to implement the strategy.

Since I was selling my business growth strategies at the time to independent grocers across the country; a meet and greet wasn't feasible for me.

I needed to replicate myself and a CD was a fabulous tool to use for that. The prospect could listen and learn about me and my services and figure out if I was a good fit for them based on my CD.

It worked very well because most of grocery store owners I spoke with were very interested in what it was I could do for them. I have a grocery background so I could speak their language.

That was a huge point, you need to speak the language of your prospects and clients. If you don't they will not trust you.

## Call to Action:

First things first; you have to something to talk about. Something your clients or prospects want to know the answer to.

Also, don't feel like you need to dump all your knowledge onto one CD or DVD. Think about one CD per subject matter. You can fit about 70 minutes onto a standard CD so that is enough time to talk intelligently on most subjects.

Going back to having a plan before you speak on a subject. If you are going to give this away for FREE do not give away all of your knowledge unless that is the plan.

Depending on your business, giving away everything will mean that your clients or prospects will no longer need you. So, if telling them everything makes them come to you more because they still don't think they can do it on their own; that's the golden ticket.

There is definitely a fine line there. You will need to plan accordingly.

If you are to sell your information which is commonly referred to as Information Marketing, then feel free to tell as much as you want to. A brain dump if you will.

We haven't discussed this yet but having the information and being an expert on a given subject is a Priceless commodity to have.

You can charge a huge amount of money for your knowledge. To give you an example; I just spent $2500 to learn about setting up a Blog and Facebook supersite.

I thought it was money well spent. The individual I invested in this from went through the entire course and took me by the hand to create this.

$2500 just to share his knowledge. Amazing right?

## Your Ideas

# STRATEGY #36

## BECOME A CELEBRITY

You can be a celebrity for many reasons. You can be scandalous, crazy, always around, funny, etc.

I bet a lot of you have local celebrities in your town who are famous for whatever reason. Look at the Kardashian's, genius right?

Becoming a celebrity will bring you opportunities that you will not have if you just stay doing what you're doing.

What does that mean?

If you are in business and you are conducting your business like you have for years and not seeking out any type of attention; that is what I mean.

Mind you, if that is what you want to do then do it. If you would want a little recognition for what you do; maybe some exposure or notoriety then this is for you.

Getting back to the opportunities you can create for yourself by being a celebrity is as follows:

1) Public speaking engagements

2) Radio/TV interviews

3) Print interviews

4) Just getting mentioned in articles, and on radio/TV as part of a discussion

5) Being spotted in public

6) People supporting your business more

7) More referrals

8) Guru status

9) Social Media engagement

10) Writing

11) Many more

## Here's an example:

There was a local home goods store that had a crazy owner who did TV commercials in the Milwaukee market. He was on TV for about a decade until he sold the business for a nice little profit.

He was called "Crazy TV Lenny". He got on camera and screamed about the deals, the freebies and the savings. It was very effective and he became a local legend.

If he was ever spotted in public, people would engage with him and that would further his celebrity with his client base.

Sales soared because of this strategy.

## Call to Action:

Keep in mind that this strategy is not for everyone. You have to be ready for it. You have to embrace it. If you don't then don't do it.

But if you do, do it and own it.

TV, radio, newspaper, magazines, writing, social media, etc. are your vehicles to celebrity.

These strategies are all separately listed in this book and might hold the key that opens up this door.

## Your Ideas

# STRATEGY #37

## GIVE BACK TO CHARITY

Charities are a hidden gem that is staring you in the face constantly. You may have never considered non-profits or charity events but think about who you can meet at these events or on these boards.

You will access to some very heavy hitters in your industry or an industry that can by an ally to yours.

What I just described is the selfish side of helping out a non-profit or charity. The "what's in it for you" philosophy which I hope you don't follow. You should have a personal interest in the cause you want to help.

Just had to clarify my position there. Everything you do should have a win-win dynamic involved in it.

Serving on a committee for a non-profit or charity can be some of the most rewarding work you can do personally. I know I have enjoyed my time helping out whenever I could.

Attending events is also very important to the success of the organization. Eating that rubber chicken is important to their continued success.

The networking that goes on at these events are also worth your while. Now it's ok to be a little selfish. When you paid to be there.

## Here's an example:

I was on the Board of Directors for my local March Of Dimes golf outing each year. I thought it was a great way to give back since my oldest brother was a "Poster Baby" for them when he was little.

If you remember I'm also in the golf business so I thought it was a win-win for everyone involved.

Not only did I get to meet several professional golfers (the outing used the Wisconsin PGA as ringers for our scramble event), I made a lot of business contacts because it was a high entry fee to play so my ideal client was right there in front of me.

Now as always the event came first and foremost. There was no question about that. But during dinner, the silent and live auctions and happy hour, it was "game on" so to speak.

This was a natural tie-in for me and it helped a worthy cause. I was happy to do it.

## Call to Action:

This is as easy as writing down what you are passionate about it.

Is it the environment, an illness, those less fortunate or some other worthy cause?

This should be a simple one for you to embrace. One word of caution though, don't get involved with so many causes that you don't have time for your business, family or friends anymore. Trust me, it's easy to do.

## Your Ideas

# STRATEGY #38

# LEVERAGE GOOGLE HANGOUTS

This is a fairly new strategy to get clients. You can turn any Hangout into a live video call. A Hangout is a video voice call similar to a webinar but everyone sees you so it's much more intimate.

You can have up to 10 clients or prospects to start a voice call from your computer or Android/Apple phones so you can connect with everyone at anytime.

Most business owners will have these scheduled just like a meeting or webinar start time. You can live stream an event this way or an information session.

This is an involving technology and may drastically change very quickly. The information I give you here could already be outdated but check it out and see if it's for you.

## Here's an example:

I literally was on a Google Hangout last night. I was listening to John Benson interview Jay Abraham. Two big names in the marketing consulting niche.

I know they had several hundred people watching them talk live and answer questions. You could see both of them because that is how Hangouts work. Plus when anyone from the virtual audience asked a question, you could see them live also. Pretty cool.

It was just like the video phones they promised us would be available in the future when I was a kid. Awesome.

I have attended a few Hangouts now and I really like how they are very present and quick to put together. You can have one in a matter of minutes or plan it out in advance to get the word out.

Now on the Hangout I was just referring to with John and Jay; it was just content and answering viewer questions. No selling at all which in the marketing world is rare.

If they wanted to however they could've sold anything and everything so it's up to you how you want to do things.

## Call to Action:

First of all go to Google and check out Hangouts and get a feel for this new technology. There are demos and scheduled events for you to experience this first hand.

Once you get a feel for it; start your lists of things to talk about. You've done this exercise before with other strategies. For me it always comes down to making a list.

I love lists because they are very concise and fairly planned out. I make mine like an outline. Lists are something I reference all of the time. I can look at my list and know exactly what to do very quickly and easily.

## Your Ideas

# STRATEGY #39

## CREATE YOUR OWN WEB TV SHOW

Web TV is a lot of work. This is a great vehicle for celebrity status. Shows can be whatever length that you like. 5 min. or an hour, it doesn't matter.

It just has to be done consistently. Each and every time you say it will be released it has to be. Nothing will kill your momentum more than missing a show time i.e. every Tuesday at 3 pm.

I led off saying this is a lot of work. I mean that most sincerely. If you don't want it to be a huge production that is okay. It can be whatever you want it to be.

If however you want it to be a huge deal with lots of cameras and editing with graphics and music then go for it.

This is a great vehicle to get noticed by others. Others meaning TV and movie execs. I know that sounds crazy but YouTube is creating stars every day.

### Here's an example:

Andrew Lock has a web TV show called "Help My Business Sucks". It's been the number one podcast on iTunes for quite a while.

Not only has Andrew done a great job creating a show but he also teaches others to do it so you can say that he has several reasons to do it.

On the show he helps businesses and also gives tips on how to do tasks faster or he gives software recommendations that help you do things easier.

He has made a great living doing his show. He gets quite a bit of money in sponsorship deals for his show plus the consulting opportunities he receives because of the show.

It's become his lead generation marketing tool.

## Call to Action:

Research your niche to see if this strategy can work for you and your business. It will require people to be interested in what it is you have to say.

The show needs to be scripted so that you sound clear and concise. You also want a HD camera so it has the best video you can offer. A microphone will help greatly also.

So… do you think you can do this? Of course you can.

## Your Ideas

# STRATEGY #40

# CREATE A WEB RADIO SHOW AND PODCASTS

This is another strategy along the line of becoming a celebrity. It will give you a platform to spread the word of your industry and your business.

It's as simple as recording your program and uploading it to one of the web radio sites on the internet. The biggest name is "Blog Talk Radio" but there are several others to choose from.

Once the program is recorded and put out to the world, it is now considered a Podcast. Maybe you have heard of Podcast's. The cool thing about Podcasts is that your information can live on for a long time so it's good for SEO.

Everything done online should factor in SEO. You want and need to be found by your clients and prospects at all times.

Getting back to your show. Most are pre-recorded and then put up online. You can have a live show if you want but then it can't be edited like you would like. Even pre-recorded programs can be scheduled then have listeners ask their questions like a live show.

## Here's an example:

Adam Carolla is best known for being Jimmy Kimmel's friend. He's a very funny comedian especially if you like inappropriate raunchy comedy. And I do.

Adam started a live radio show on the internet called the "Adam Carolla Show". He was syndicated on regular radio and I don't know what happened there but he has switched to an internet show and is killing it.

## Call to Action:

Well I have turned into a broken record on this by now but you have to look into this strategy to see how you can leverage this into an advantage for you.

I believe you can turn any business into an internet radio show that can bring clients in.

You can use your FreeConferenceCall.com account to create your show so the investment is very low.

One last thing, try to have only one message per episode so that it's very consistent and concise.

## Your Ideas

# STRATEGY #41

# HELP OTHERS IN FORUMS

Forum's are a place where you go to get very specific questions answered. It's a place for nerds, lurkers, haters and those who need help.

One thing is for sure though, everyone there is interested in that topic. They are passionate about the subject matter. For some it's a hobby, others are all in. It's life and death for them.

And for me, I just want my question answered and usually someone beat me to it so I just read the answers and find the one that makes the most sense to me.

There is a forum set up for any topic and subject matter you can think of. From cars to dating to fetishes. You name it, they have it.

Forum's are also a great place to acquire clients and prospects also. Since forums are set up to be a place where you can flex your intellectual muscle with your knowledge of a certain topic, it's a great place to offer your products or services for others to get more information.

Just don't get flamed. Getting flamed is when you get called out or warned or banned from the site for spamming others with your website address or buying information.

You can do it but there is a protocol. First it can't look self-serving. You need to give good information that is useful to the readers and then you can suggest for them to go to a website for additional information as long as it doesn't appear to be yours.

Confusing right? So pick a username that is ambiguous and not something associated with your business name or website address. As long as it looks like you are giving out friendly information, you will be fine.

## Here's an example:

Gary Vaynerchuk started Wine Library TV a few years ago. It was a video wine review site that also promoted his father's wine store in a very non-obvious way. He was careful about this.

Well to get viewers and to further his personal brand; Gary would search out wine forums to help the users there figure out wine pairings and any other wine questions they might have.

He became an authority on many sites and he also gave people his web address for further information to learn about wine.

Gary was very careful not to get flamed. He of course learned this the hard way because he got banned quickly on a few sites for spamming.

When he figured out the rules of forums, he rocked it hard. He grew his personal brand, his Wine Library TV site and his dad's liquor store also.

It was one of the greatest strategies he found that worked for him. This was because Gary loves people and he wanted to help them.

Pretty simple right??

## Call to Action:

Writing is a very non-threatening way to get your communication and your knowledge out there for others to see. It's why "Haters" or "Trolls" take to the internet and spew their vomit about others to all that will listen.

Look up forums in your business niche and start reading the posts there. Can you help those who need questions asked?

I bet you can. You will be amazed at how good you will feel afterwards especially if the person asking the question thanks you for helping them.

I think that is why so many people are on forums. They want to help and they like to feel good that they helped someone. I know you will too.

## Your Ideas

# STRATEGY #42

## LEVERAGE FISH BOWLS AND RAFFLES

We all have seen them, fish bowls and raffles. After all these years, they still work marvelously.

A fish bowl is a container meant to gather business cards. They are usually spotted at the counter of a restaurant meant to give away a FREE lunch if your card is picked out of the bowl.

It's a great way to build your client list if it's at your restaurant because they are already clients.

It's a good way to build a prospect list if the fish bowl is at another business and you are trying to get their clients over to your business.

Raffles are a wild card because you can do them several different ways. You can give away an item at your store and have a raffle for your clients only.

You can go big and give away a car and have this raffle be a national lead generation building platform for you.

As always, what you do with the information gathered is the key to this. If you do nothing with entries, business cards and leads then don't bother. It's a waste of time and money.

If however, you plan a strategic sales process around your new prospects for them to get to know you better; now we're talking.

I have found raffles to be a very good way to find new clients for my Putting Green business. I ask very specific questions once they enter in their personal information.

They are leading questions meant to give me an indication if they will be a buyer to me in the future or if they will just be interested in the raffle prize.

Here is an example of what I'm talking about.

--Do you wish you could play or practice golf more often?

--Do you have children that enjoy playing golf or would love to learn?

--Would you like more information on having a having a Putting Green at your home?

Simple "yes/no" questions that indicate where their mind is at. I encourage you to do the same. People will always give you more information than you think they will.

## Here's an example:

I'm going to continue on with my example of a raffle.

The information I gather for my raffles has been wonderful.

I ask them for their personal information like name, address, phone, etc. The normal information needed for me to contact them.

I also ask them for their age, if they own a home, if they have children, etc.

This gives me all the information I need to see if they fit my desired avatar that I mentioned earlier in this book.

I do not ask about gender or race because that is irrelevant to me and I feel that has nothing to do with my business and can only label me as something that I'm not.

I take the information given to me and enter it into my database of prospects to follow up with. I have a marketing funnel in place to take care of my new prospects.

If the prospect doesn't want information on a Putting Green business, that is ok with me. I'm happy to not spend time, money and energy with someone who will not be a buyer. Harsh maybe but necessary. They just did you a favor. They respected your time, money and energy. You should thank them.

## Call to Action:

How can you have a fish bowl or a raffle that will bring you business?

For me it starts with a list. You've heard this before right?

You can have a raffle at your store or you can have a raffle through your newsletter or email correspondence. It's really up to you how you want to do it and how you want to control it.

Items that are good to give away are products that have value. Your time if you consult. Autographed Memorabilia is always a hit. Restaurant gift certificates are popular. Anything and everything you can think of really. If it has perceived value then someone will want to win it.

Contact strategic alliances. Remember them? They probably wouldn't mind giving away something FREE to their clients that didn't cost them anything. You will be surprised by the response you will get from that alone.

So... who do you know who wants to give away FREE stuff?

## Your Ideas

# STRATEGY #43

# EXHIBIT AT FAIRS OR FESTIVALS

Fairs and festivals are a crap shoot. I say this because you don't know who is coming.

It's not like a tradeshow where there is a specific niche or industry you can plan for.

Fairs and festivals are meant for the entire community to enjoy. It could be a local town's fair or maybe a county or state fair. You have to plan accordingly.

They can also be set up on a theme like health fairs or a festival that is a fundraiser to help pay medical bills.

These are great if your business is built around consumables like food and drink. They might also be good if you are in political field or a consumer awareness business. Then you want a melting pot of people.

Niche businesses need to evaluate the fair and festival on who will be attending, where the event is and if it works for their personal schedule.

I will add one last thing. If you are a local retail business and the fair is a local event, you should strongly consider being there. The attendees are your clients. It will be good to get that exposure for your business. You will be amazed at how many people didn't even know your business existed.

## Here's an example:

My brother Mike owns a Chicago Style Hot Dog restaurant in a small town north of Milwaukee called "WOW Dog".

His local community has a Cherry Festival once a year at the local park. This is a natural fit for my brother because he has a consumable product that people will expect to find at festivals; Hot Dogs.

He also has a restaurant in this community that he can leverage to get new clients for himself. Win- Win

And another thing he has going for him is that at the festival, there are thousands of people descending upon one small park and that means a lot of potential hot dog sales.

My brother is smart for being a part of this every year. It has really helped his business and I know he looks forward to it each and every year.

## Call to Action:

Look locally for a listing of fairs and festivals. Believe it or not you will probably find this listing and if you research it enough, you probably will also find a tradeshow for all of the vendors who want to participate at the fairs.

We have one locally in Milwaukee where there is a booth for local bands, local security firms, ad specialty companies, food vendors, you name they are there.

Pick the fair or festival that makes the most sense for you. If it's themed you will have a great indication of who will come. If it's local you might want to consider that also.

Remember this is about getting leads and educating the attendees with literature, etc.

Don't try to sell unless of course you have products that can be carried off easily. Think jewelry not Hot Tubs.

I feel I have to say this; if you have Hot Tubs, that's ok but you will have to schedule the installation. People will not put one on their backs and carry it off. LOL

## Your Ideas

# STRATEGY #44

## DEVELOP DOOR TO DOOR SALES AND LEADS

I know this sounds like something you might see from the stone ages but this still works. Most people when this is mentioned will cringe but I'll try to make it palatable.

If you are old enough you may remember door to door salesman. They were selling encyclopedia's and vacuum cleaners. I remember both giving presentations to my mom. If I remember correctly she bought a vacuum cleaner from someone.

Believe it not there is still a tremendous amount of business done at the front doors of homes. Today in most municipalities you will need to have a permit to do so but it may be worth considering.

On a daily basis you will still find kids selling a fundraising product, home improvement sales people, religious groups, politicians and cable/satellite companies all trying to get your attention and your money.

### Here's an example:

The Girl Scouts of America has this system nailed down. They sell cookies once a year and they sell millions of them by knocking on neighbors doors. Who can resist them?

Every neighborhood has several girls who go out and sell-sell-sell.

They have a very simple sales script. It goes something like this:

--*Would you like to buy some Girl Scout Cookies?*

No price, no nothing... and it works

## Call to Action:

You probably can't compete with the Girl Scouts. Not many companies can. They are awesome but this can work for you.

I have considered this on more than one occasion but never pulled the trigger on it.

Here is what I was going to do and maybe this might help you. Keep in mind I am selling Putting Greens that the investment in one is around $4000-$6000.

I was going to hire college kids in the summer to target high end subdivisions to go door to door and bring me appointments. They would capture the interested parties name and phone number with address and what exactly were they interested in.

It would've been a survey that was sponsored by my company and all they were doing was asking questions.

Here were some of them:

--*Do you have a back yard entertainment area?*

*If you don't mind me asking, what does your area consist of?*

*Grill, Deck, Patio, Pool, Trampoline, Swing set, etc.*

So the survey was the vehicle I was going to use to get leads. By the way if the homeowner would've wanted information on a deck or anything else on the list, I would've found a resource for them and got paid for it.

So develop a purpose for what it is you want to accomplish. Do you want leads, sales, awareness or something else?

Keep in mind, you don't have to do this yourself. You can hire this out and I recommend that you do.

# Your Ideas

# STRATEGY #45

## LEVERAGE TELE-SEMINARS

Teleseminars aren't as popular as they used to be but can still be very effective.

I think this is because there are new "bright shiny objects" that have come along. Those being Google Hangouts and Webinars as mentioned earlier in the book.

I think teleseminars are perfect for introverts who want to put out great information but don't need to be on video. They just want to talk and hide behind a microphone in anonymity.

I can understand this completely.

A teleseminar is a phone call amongst clients and prospects. You schedule this with your contacts for a given date and time or you can also advertise this to get new prospects. You all meet at that time on your phones and you speak while they listen.

Pretty simple really. You can use your FreeConferenceCall.com account.

Once you do the teleseminar, you can replay it or turn it into a podcast and upload it to iTunes.

# Here's an example:

I have done a bunch of these over the years. I had a consulting business a few years back that catered to independent grocers.

I did a different topic every week for about 12 weeks. I invited my clients and prospects to attend so they could listen and ask questions at the end of the call.

The goal was to create an information product to sell to them at a later date that could help their businesses.

I had guests that were more expert than me on the calls depending on the topic we covered. Most of the time these experts had products or services that could extend to my grocer clients to make life easier or to push more groceries through the registers.

Overall it was a success and that series of information helped my clients. All I did was burn the audio file to a CD and sell them.

# Call to Action:

Pick a topic you are comfortable talking about and create a script for what you were going to say.

I used to script out the opening and say it word for word so that I sounded professional and intelligent to my listeners. I would then use bullet points to talk about the topics I would be covering.

If I had a guest on I would get questions from the guest that I was supposed to ask and in the order I was to ask them. This is important because the guest wants to be viewed as someone who is professional and intelligent also.

You can always do the first one without anyone listening and see how you do. If it's good you can either upload it to your website or to iTunes. Or you can burn it to a CD and sell it.

If you don't like it, you can edit it or redo it with the corrections you would like to make.

Listen for your tone. What I mean by that is you should be talking with a smile on. You should be upbeat and enthusiastic. This doesn't mean over the top like Robin Williams but not boring either.

You want your clients and prospects to listen to the end. That is where you will make your offer if you have one and create sales for yourself.

## Your Ideas

# STRATEGY #46

## LEVERAGE NEW MOVERS

New movers are just that; people who have moved into your area of town. They say that people have a tendency to move every five years on average. If you are in a more transient part of town where there a lot of apartments or duplexes than those numbers might be higher.

This strategy is for retailers and restaurants mostly. Anyone with an online business will not care about their clients address but brick and mortar businesses will.

Think about what you go through when you moved into a new area of town. You probably had to find a new dry cleaners, a new auto mechanic, maybe a new doctor or dentist. It is much more than moving furniture and boxes.

There are companies that will provide with a list of those who have just moved into your area. If you are a local auto mechanic this can be very beneficial to you because the majority of people tend to go to mechanics that are near their homes.

If you can capture those individuals before they would even try someone else then you got them for as long as they live in your area.

That's cool and profitable for you.

# Here's an example:

My friend Pat Pendergast has a company called "Welcome Card USA". It specializes in New Movers and he creates a marketing plan around these movers.

Pat figures that you need to contact new movers within the first 60 days of their initial move. Anything after that has a much larger diminishing return. This is because after 60 days the new mover has their area figured out enough to make their own decisions.

Depending on the business he consults with, he always suggests giving away something for FREE or at a deep discount. It's his opinion that if you get these new neighbors into your business. you have a great opportunity to land them as a regular client. He's absolutely correct.

He has told me of an auto mechanic that was able to get six new clients in one month because of this campaign. It cost the mechanic an oil change which is the garages low cost leader for new clients anyway.

By giving away six oil changes, Pat's client received over $2000 in new business.

Let me explain, most people don't have an understanding of how their cars work and what goes wrong with them. Put me on that list too.

They think all they have to do is turn the key and put gas in it once in a while. It's not their faults entirely, most people were trained this way.

So getting back to Pat's client. The mechanic found something on each car that needed immediate attention and he was able to convince his new clients that it would be in their best interests to fix the problems.

A good mechanic knows when things need to be replaced and when things need to be watched. This was a good mechanic.

# Call to Action:

Can a New Mover campaign work for you? If you are in a high traffic, highly competitive business then of course.

If you are one of only three tropical fish stores in your city then maybe not.

It's important to know where your clients come from. Are they mostly local or do your clients tend to travel a ways to get to your location?

Once you figure this out then you can move on or move in so to speak.

Can you make them an irresistible offer to come try you out? Remember that people like to date or audition their new businesses. They are wary. They like to be cautious.

You can thank your predecessors for this lack of trust.

## Your Ideas

# STRATEGY #47

# BECOME A SPONSOR

Sponsoring sports teams, special events and buildings have become the norm over the last 10 years. You may not have millions of dollars to do it like the big companies do it, but you can do it on a small scale locally.

Local sponsorship has also been very common over the years. Companies get listed on all of the print and media material for whatever the event is or whatever the shirt the softball team wears.

This has been a sneaky way to advertise and give back to your community. This definitely falls into the win-win-win side of doing business.

The event or team wins because much needed money is given. The company wins because their business gets a lot of attention. The public wins because now there is a better event or a better league to play in.

I will always promote this type of doing business.

## Here's an example:

We have a local attorney who is the single biggest advertiser in the Milwaukee market for any type of business. He now is sponsoring run/walks and sports teams. He is a very shrewd advertiser.

The cost to print shirts is nominal because the more you print the less expensive it is.

What he cleverly has figured out is that he has taken the best spot on both sides of the shirt for his firm. He is prominently displayed.

But the pure genius of this strategy is that the public will continue to wear these shirts over and over again in public. Giving him a constant bill board associated with a positive activity in the community.

Not bad for an attorney. Just kidding. Sort of.

## Call to Action:

What can you get involved with? What is near and dear to you? What will help your business? What will make you look like a player in the community?

Just keep asking yourself some very simple questions like those and you will find your answer.

This won't be for you if you are struggling right now. Take care of business first. This will fall on the side of giving back once you have extra money to do something with. That isn't an absolute but it's a good generality.

The different things you can sponsor are sports teams, live events, special programs, anything community related and even business services.

That's right business services can be sponsored. If you are a printer who hasn't asked you for a break on printing allowing you to put your print shop on the paper as a sponsor.

This may be for you if you don't have a checkbook where you can write a check. There are companies who put information out or do live events that need services provided to pull these events off. You can become a sponsor to that business and discount your product or offer it for FREE if it makes sense for you to do so.

Getting some ideas now?

## Your Ideas

# PART 1 - SUMMARY

I just did a brain dump of massive proportions on you. Some of these strategies will revolutionize your business in ways you can't imagine. Other strategies won't work for you and others will have modest success.

Someone once said "I don't know one way to get 72 new clients but I know 72 ways to get 1 client". Profound isn't it? I have a real life example for you on how this exact notion worked for me this week alone.

I did five different Putting Green quotes this week. Monday the client was a referral. Tuesday the client found me on the internet. Wednesday was from Facebook. Thursday was an existing client and Friday was from a tradeshow. I couldn't make this up if I tried.

If these strategies can work for me in a very niche business, it can certainly work for you.

Please consider all of these strategies because you will never know what will work for you until you actually do it.

You also won't know if you would personally like a strategy until you do it. Obviously there will be strategies that just the thought of them will make you cringe for one reason or another. Skip those.

The key to this book and these strategies is for you to do something.

Author Robert Ringer wrote a book that explains this to a tee. Its title is:

ACTION! Nothing Happens Until Something Moves

Perfect... And so true.

Honestly, your business is yours to do whatever you would like to do with it. You own it. I just want you to own it in the way you envisioned it would be when you started it or when you bought it.

For some of you it has become a job. You might not have a boss anymore but it's not exactly what you thought it would be. Change that.

So do yourself a favor and give something a try. Just do one of them and see how it goes. They all work but not if you don't do anything about it.

Try to start with strategies that will leverage your time and your money first. Always consider what is the best use of both of these and you minimize your failure right from the start.

Don't forget about the FREE Quick Start Guide and Webinar to get you going along the right path.

It's also a great way to find comfort in the fact that you are not alone anymore. There are others like you who also want to succeed and might have some questions along the way.

Shoot me an email and tell me about it. Let me know how it's going. Tell me your wins and your losses. If I can help I will.

Jim@StrategicBusinessBreakthroughs.com

# Part Two

# More Often

Part two is all about having your clients come back to you more often. It doesn't matter if you have an online store or if you have a brick and mortar business.

Repeat sales are vital to your success. It's what will make you successful and potentially RICH.

Part one dealt with new clients and the different ways to find them and acquire them. It's the lifeblood of any business.

Now we need those same clients to keep coming back to continue to support their needs and desires. As much as you want this to be about you, it's about them.

You have a duty to keep offering products and services that your clients want and need.

Some of these strategies in this section are the same as in part one. It's because they are that important to each part of the "More Clients...More Often...More Money" process.

I would suggest that if you see a strategy from part one mentioned again in part two; pay extra attention to it. Make sure you implement it because it is that vital.

Look for this symbol(*). This symbol means money in your bank.

# STRATEGY #48

## OFFER STRONG GUARANTEES*

Guarantees allow for existing clients to buy with confidence. Remember the public is very skeptical of businesses and they need to feel safe with them. Offering strong guarantees is the best way to keep your clients happy and coming back for more.

The longer the guarantee the more comfortable your client is. Craftsman tools have a lifetime guarantee. I have a few of them because of the guarantee alone. A lifetime guarantee is the best guarantee you can offer.

Guarantees and return policies scare business owners. They think the public will take advantage of them with this type of guarantee. This is bad thinking.

How many times have you returned something the last day you could because the receipt said you had 10 days to do it by? I know I have.

If that business would've put a longer time on the receipt I probably would've kept it because I would have forgotten about the return policy.

Do not let a couple of your clients who may abuse your return policies or your guarantees let you dictate a bad business decision.

They really aren't your clients anyway. They're probably cherry pickers and you shouldn't waste your time with them.

## Here's an example:

It is common in the marketing consulting world to offer lifetime guarantees on the products that these gurus offer for sale.

They know that if there is a lifetime guarantee attached to the sale of their product, they will sell more. They also know that their returns will go down.

Now, obviously everything in that arena is not a lifetime guarantee because some consultants deal exclusively with the internet and that changes almost daily so yesterdays information may be outdated in six months. But even they offer a strong guarantee to make their clients more comfortable with their purchases.

## Call to Action:

How long of a guarantee can you offer? How strong of a guarantee can you offer? Write down what you can do and what it would look like if you doubled it.

What does that mean by doubling it? Can you extend your warranty or guarantee by twice as much time? Two years instead of One? Can you offer double your money back if not completely satisfied?

Interesting questions aren't they? Gets you thinking. How many of my clients would actually take me up on my guarantee? 1%, 5%, 10% or more?

It's been proven over and over and in every possible industry. The stronger your guarantee, return policy or warranty you offer the more sales you will gain and the less returns you will have.

I am assuming of course that you offer a quality product or service and that you are not a conman.

## Your Ideas

# STRATEGY #49

## COMMUNICATE ON A MORE PERSONAL LEVEL WITH YOUR CLIENTS*

Communication is completely in your control. That's the cool part because you can deliver a very specific message whenever you desire.

The key to this strategy is to deliver a consistent message and on a consistent time frame. Inconsistency is as good as doing nothing.

I know what you're thinking. You are afraid of bombarding your clients with too many messages. You see other companies do it and you hate that.

Have you ever noticed that those companies that you hate are only jamming sales messages down your throat? They are not giving you any valuable information.

Communicating more frequently by itself isn't necessarily the right way of doing things unless you include communicating more effectively. These two strategies are intertwined with each other.

This strategy is about communicating on a more personal level. You shouldn't treat your clients all the same. Your best clients should be treated the best. They should get different offers than your other clients and they will respond in kind.

You do need to let them know that you are giving this offer to them because of how special they are to you. Otherwise they will think that everyone gets the same deal.

The key to this strategy is also to let your clients know more about you as a person. Let them into your lives a little bit. Whatever you are comfortable with.

People respond to those that they believe they know. People they believe they are friends with. Even if it's because they read it. They will grow more attached to you.

## Here's an example:

We have a local businesswoman in Milwaukee who has recently gone through some tough times medically. In fact her medical condition is only going to get worse and not better.

She originally kept this to herself because it was a personal issue and she didn't want to burden her clients with her problems.

One day she decided to let her best clients in on her secret. She didn't know how they would respond  because everyone has problems that they deal with every day.

Much to her surprise her clients rallied around her. They offered tips to help her cope and have a better quality of life. They shared their personal stories. They came together as a community for her.

And her business hasn't suffered for it either. In fact it is doing better than ever. She couldn't be happier that she let people into her life.

## Call to Action:

Please don't feel you have to share personal and intimate information on your life to your clients. You can share your experiences you had at the grocery store check out if you think it has relevance somehow.

The best way to communicate more frequently and more effectively is to schedule your communication.

Create a marketing calendar where all of your communication is scheduled. Get a year-long calendar and mark down when your sales will be. When you will send out educational material. When you will send out your newsletter.

Don't worry about sending out too much material. If it has value to your client then they will embrace it.

Can you see where this will allow you to be more consistent with your message and be more effective?

All I ask you to do is make your messages a little more personal. Maybe mix in a story of an experience you just had. Something that a lot of people can relate to.

That's all. Keep it simple.

## Your Ideas

# STRATEGY #50

## CREATE A WARM WELCOMING ENVIRONMENT FOR YOUR CLIENTS

This applies to both online and offline businesses. Everyone can be more welcoming. It's easier to think of a retailer with this strategy because that is more tangible.

As a retailer, what can you offer to your clients when they come into your store? Coffee, wine, cookies, attention?

That last word; attention. Interesting right? It's much more than saying "May I help you? It's about engaging with your clients in a more personal way.

Maybe it's a piece of jewelry they are wearing or a pair of shoes they have on. It could be their vehicle if you noticed it or their hair style. There is always a sincere compliment you can offer to get your client to feel more comfortable and welcomed.

Don't mistake this with manipulation. Because if you are not sincere it will appear to be very hollow and make people uncomfortable.

You want to start a dialogue with your clients. One preferably that is centered around them. It's been proven over and over again that people like to talk about themselves.

If you are online only. This can be done also. It's much less intimate and you need to be more creative about it.

First of all you need to make everything easily accessible to your returning visitors. Make everything easy to find and make the checkout process as easy as possible.

If you can do those two things you will be in great shape for a return visit.

## Here's an example:

There is a local restaurant that does this spectacularly. It's a family owned Italian restaurant that has been there for two generations.

They start by asking if you have ever been there before. If you haven't they go through the restaurants history and how the family recipes are used in every dish. It's a great story. It immediately draws you in.

If you have been there before and they recognize you, they give you a hug or a big hello to welcome you back.

The restaurant does a great job at engaging the client and making them feel welcomed. The client feels like they belong there and go back more often because they are treated like family.

## Call to Action:

This is a personal one because it will mostly come from you. Inside of you. It isn't about product choices you carry, it's about personality and a little choreography.

What I mean by choreography is how you have your store set up and how you walk a client through the sales process or through your store.

You truly need to see your store or your website through the eyes of your clients. Try to see things from their perspective. It will be enlightening.

I have had clients see things that truly embarrassed them like cob webs or trash that may have been there for a long time.

I have also had clients feel pride because they took a moment to reflect on all the good they do and continue to do.

So take a moment and really think about your clients and their experiences with you and your staff. Look for what you are doing well with and what you need to enhance upon.

This will not be a 5 minute exercise. This could take a few hours. For some a few days if not more.

Be honest with yourselves. You'll be better off.

## Your Ideas

# STRATEGY #51

## OFFER FAVORABLE PRICING WHEN YOUR CLIENTS PURCHASE MORE

Think Sam's Club and Costco. Why sell one pair of socks when three pairs are better. They are the Kings of bundling more products together.

This world has revolved around volume discounts. Your vendors give you better pricing the more you buy from them and you should do the same for your clients.

Easy concept and there are many ways to accomplish this with your clients.

Let me show you a few that will show you what I mean:

--Discounts for buying more than one. You've all seen "save $2 when you buy three" right?

--Reward punch cards. Sub shops have done this for years. "Buy six subs get the 7th free".

--Mixing and matching different types of the same product. This is used if you buy multiple colors of the same item. Think socks again.

-- You buy more and pass the savings on to your clients. This is by far the most common way this strategy is done. And the more they buy the more they save.

## Here's an example:

Subways for years have had punch cards. Since they are independently owned, not all of them offer them. The one I go to does.

You buy six subs and you get a FREE six inch sub Free on your 7th visit. Pretty simple concept. The business card they had printed up didn't cost much and it was a simple design.

It was enough to keep me loyal to get my FREE sub. I didn't go to another Subway or to another sub shop. I kept going back to the same one until I got my FREE sub.

This fits into this strategy because the subs were cheaper if you took into account the FREE one at the end. I had to wait to see the benefit but I still got it.

If you bought seven subs from that Subway, they were the cheapest because of the FREE one.

This same Subway also ran promotions that if you bought two foot long subs you got the third one FREE. Another great promotion because I did this one too. My wife and I would get the three foot longs between us and that would be two meals.

They had us locked in.

## Call to Action:

What can you offer to encourage more buying?

Is it cheaper pricing if your clients buy more? Maybe it's better pricing if they buy so much over a course of time like a rebate.

There are countless options for you to decide on. Maybe you will have multiple programs based on the product itself.

Some products are consumable like food and drink. Some are disposed of quicker than others like paper towels and toilet paper.

Others need to be replaced every so often like socks and underwear. Well they should anyway. LOL

Think about your products and they might speak to you for you.

## Your Ideas

# STRATEGY #52

## TRAIN YOUR CLIENTS WITH EDUCATION

Most people hate school but they like to learn. Educating your clients is about teaching and learning. The good not the bad.

If someone goes to your website or into your store, they have an interest in what it is you do.

Chances are they want more information about your industry to better educate themselves and become a better client and better consumer.

I see this all the time especially in certain industries like health and wellness. Consumers are sponges to learn all they can about their bodies and how they can look better and feel better.

It is your responsibility to educate them. Do not just sell them something without making sure they made the best decision possible for them.

To some that sounds ridiculous. To others it makes total sense.

If you own a convenience store and sell tobacco, alcohol, bubble gum and soda to people, I get that reasoning. But what if a portion of your store had healthier alternatives and you took the time to mention it to your clients at the time of purchase. Would you make a difference with some? Would that make a difference to the thinking of some of them or to you?

It really can be a slippery slope because it's possible to sound like a preacher vs. an educator.

This will offend some but a preacher will turn people away while an educator will bring people in. No one likes to be preached to.

## Here's an example:

Jay Abraham calls this the "Strategy of Preeminence". It's where you care so much for your clients; their well being, their lives, everything.

He uses an example of someone who sells glasses of water to the public. He mentions that he could sell a glass of water all day long and not think anything of it.

He also mentions a "what if".

"What if" he was to educate each person on how much water they should drink in a given day for optimum health and looks.


"What if" he was to mention the different qualities of water you could choose from.

"What if" he refused to sell a glass of water to anyone without telling them about the benefits of water.

Yes this example is about a glass of water just like the one out of your tap at home. He wanted to use a simple example just to prove a point that if you can take a glass of water and make it important, what can you do with your products and services.

## Call to Action:

Start by making a list of your products features and benefits.

A feature is a car being white in color. A benefit is that it will be cooler in the summer sun.

Once you have your list start by creating talking points using your features and benefits. You can script this into a presentation if you'd like but it's not necessary if you aren't formally presenting your products to clients.

This is a good strategy to remember that in your own personal life; you've had good sales presentations and bad sales presentations. Chances are you bought from the good presentations because you were educated and you felt confident with the knowledge you obtained that you were making a sound decision.

This is no different. Now you are the educator. You are in control. So take charge.

One last thing I want to mention here that I have left out. This strategy also encompasses how you want to run your business from the client perspective.

What does that mean?

You need to train your clients on how you want your business to run. If you want your clients to only contact you through your website or through texting or social media; you need to tell them and guide them. Otherwise they will assume you are 24/7/365 and that may not be what you want.

## Your Ideas

# STRATEGY #53

## DEVELOP A BACK-END OF
## PRODUCTS OR SERVICES

This is the strategy that can make or break your business. It's extremely important to have other items you can offer your clients.

A back-end is considered anything you offer your clients to purchase once they made the initial purchase from you. You have probably done this without knowing there was a term for it.

My hope is that you will see it as more important to do after reading this.

Once a client buys from you they will most likely need something else that compliments that purchase. A back-end sale is also a sale made to your client on a different visit or date.

Technically if it's a sale on the same date it would be a cross-sell or up-sell. We will get to those in a later strategy.

Plus as an added bonus, once your clients trust you and they will; you will be able to offer them quite a few different products for them to consider at a later date.

This goes for you service providers also. There are always much needed services you can provide after your original purchase.

## Here's an example:

Many years ago I sold insurance. I was handed vacant accounts to help me build my client base up. These vacant accounts were created from other agents who left the company and these clients needed an agent to handle their needs.

Most clients had auto and homeowners coverage which is an industry standard. Most however didn't have a personal umbrella plan. An umbrella plan typically is a one million dollar liability plan that goes on top of your present auto and homeowners coverage.

If you have anything at all to lose, this is a must have plan.

My goal was to offer this coverage to these vacant accounts as a back-end product because I could show them the need for it through education.

I was successful 50% of the time at providing my new clients with the much needed insurance. It should never be about the cost but it is if you don't take the time to educate first.

## Call to Action:

So what can you offer your clients as a back-end product or service?

If you do massages, can you offer a couples massage or a hot stone massage?

If you sell fine china and stemware, can you offer wine glasses of the same pattern that your clients bought as champagne glasses?

If you sell golf clubs, can you offer the woods that would complement the irons your client just purchased?

There is always something you can do. The biggest challenge I had when selling Putting Greens was to find an additional product to offer my clients. I started with a maintenance plan that I offered and that worked great.

Keep in mind also, this is not a onetime back-end offer. It is your responsibility to offer products and services to your clients on a regular basis. In fact you owe it to them to have the best life they possibly can by purchasing your product or service.

You can definitely make that case if you are a massage therapist right? Or how about a realtor who keeps coming across a home that would be ideal for their clients' family situation?

Are you seeing the possibilities? This can be someone else's product too. It doesn't have to be only yours. Remember the section on JV's?

## Your Ideas

# STRATEGY #54

## CREATE A FOLLOW UP SALES AND MARKETING FUNNEL

I can't tell you how many businesses I run across that have no follow up. Nada, Nothing, Zilch.

I can't help but think to myself; no wonder they're closing.

Yes, follow up systems are easiest and one of the strongest ways to make tons of money. This is a big one. If you do nothing else with this book; this is the one thing you should do.

Follow up systems can be as easy as putting together an email list to email to or a phone list to make phone calls to or an address to send mail to.

It can also be a very complex system surrounded by a marketing calendar and a sales funnel. A funnel that is different for leads, for clients, and for VIP Clients.

I hope you choose the latter but you also have to start somewhere. Don't feel that you have to create a huge system because I said so. Build it gradually. You will notice a difference immediately.

Follow up is all about ongoing communication with your clients and prospects. Not doing it is the biggest mistake businesses make when running their business. Hands Down.

Too many owners think that their clients will keep coming back on their own because they love you. They won't. At least not as often as they could or would.

Following up shows your clients and prospects that you care and that will get them to visit your website or store more often.

## Here's an example:

I have two examples for this one. The first is one is what not to do. The second is the correct way to follow up with your clients.

I was at my neighborhood grocery store and I heard the phone ring. The customer service desk where phone calls to the store come in answered the phone and it went something like this:

"our floral person is not in right now, can you call back in about 30 min.?"

Does anyone see the problem? Here you have a prospect that wants information or maybe place an order and she was told to call back. People just don't do that anymore. They go to the next store in line and give them the business.

The customer service person could've also taken down a name and phone number so as to not lose that potential business. But, no they shooed away a client.

Do you remember a strategy on training clients to make more sales?

The next example comes from my local car dealership. I do have to admit that the dealership doesn't do the follow up however, the sales rep does. It's no wonder why he doubles the sales of everyone else.

We bought a VW Jetta a few years back and to be honest my friend was the sales manager and our price was already set. My friend turned us over to his top salesman because he knew this salesman would take care of us.

Even though the salesman knew it was already a closed sale, he walked us through every feature on the car, let us test drive it, showed us the service area, etc.

Class act and what was more impressive was all of the "stick" tactics and follow up he used since the sale.

"Stick" tactics is when you do something to follow up immediately after the sale. It's meant to subside buyers remorse.

He sent us a nice card thanking us for the purchase and giving us a coupon for a FREE oil change at the service department.

This did two things. It made us use the coupon because it was a FREE oil change that we had to do anyway and it got us into the dealership to use their services which was very smart also.

Before we received the thank you card we received a personal phone call asking us if the car was running ok and if we needed help with any of the features. Smart move.

Since the purchase we have received birthday and Christmas cards along with special offers for the service department and of course a new car.

And the rest of the sales staff wonders how he is the top salesman every month. Well, I don't.

## Call to Action:

Have you already got a follow up system? Can it be tweaked to be better? Can you add anything to it?

This is too important not to do. I really believe your business depends upon a good follow up system.

Start with a simple sales funnel. If a lead comes in what steps can you put into place to walk them through education and a sale?

How can you continue to educate and make offers to your clients? Remember this is a different sales funnel because they have purchased from you already and are familiar with you.

You can do a sales funnel two ways, you can have very little content and offers or you can have many educational pieces and offers.

Remember that once you create the content you can keep reusing it over and over.

## Your Ideas

# STRATEGY #55

# DEVELOP MONTHLY CONTINUITY

How would you like your bank accounts filled up with money every first of the month? You Do? I thought you might.

Continuity is the way to do that. Think about car loans, membership fees, health clubs, etc.

Think continuous when you talk about continuity. Continuous money coming into your business is good.

Almost every business can implement this income stream. It's smart business if you can start it.

Health clubs are a simple example of continuity. On the first of each month they draw money out of your bank account "x" number of dollars whether you use the facility or not.

They are banking on the fact that you won't use the facility that much and you won't cancel your account anytime soon.

Think about every bill you pay each month. Some services you use and some you are paying for no good reason at all.

Isn't continuity great?

# Here's an example:

As good as health clubs are, there are also great business models you can model yourselves after.

Paid newsletters come to mind. I have subscribed for years to Dan Kennedy's marketing newsletter.

I mentioned earlier about Dan Kennedy. He's a genius and his newsletter is worth every penny I spend.

He has built up his newsletter over the years to what it is now but I want you to think about these numbers:

25,000 subscribers paying $40-60 per month for the newsletter. A bunch of those subscribers have signed up for his next level of membership of $249 per month

Not sure if you've done the math or not but he is at 1-1.5 million per month in continuity income.

Not too shabby.

Plus he brings in experts from fields of marketing that he is not an expert in. They do it for the exposure and he does it to offer more knowledge.

Any remember JV's and Strategic Alliances from earlier in the book?

# Call to Action:

What can you do that your clients would pay a monthly fee for?

This is a creative exercise so write down options for yourself. If you have a consumable like food and drink you can offer something like get $40 of food and drink for $30 per month plus you'll get member only benefits that no one else will be able to enjoy.

That ties a client in to coming to your store each and every month and not your competitor. That is just one example that can be mixed and matched with other industries.

To make this worthwhile to you and your clients, your offer will have to be good. If it is just ok then only your hard core best clients will take you up on it because they are probably spending it now anyway.

Remember back to the irresistible offer you created earlier in this book.

## Your Ideas

# STRATEGY #56

## HOLD SPECIAL EVENTS FOR YOUR PREFERRED CLIENTS*

Preferred/Member events are a way to get your clients excited for something. They are meant for your VIP's to feel special like they are part of something unique.

This is a great way to be creative. Your clients will love it and respond. Clients love to feel like they're being treated special.

As an added benefit to you, you will notice that your "average" clients will want to ascend to be your Preferred clients. It's human nature to want to be considered in the inner circle or members of a special club.

### Here's an example:

At the marketing seminars I attend there are always a special dinner hosted by the seminar promoter. These dinners are attended by the promoters best clients.

Those not in the inner circle always want to peak behind the curtain to see who is attending and what everyone is talking about.

The buzz is always "are you going to the dinner?" Those who chose to not be in the VIP group always regretted it at the events.

It's also not a coincidence that the ones who go to these dinners are the promoters best clients and the clients who are the most successful.

## Call to Action:

A marketing calendar can really help you out. Remember it is a calendar that lists all of your marketing tasks, roll-outs, campaigns and events. It's not an hourly schedule like a planner, it's a giant overview of your plan.

So plan for an event or a special day that you can embrace easily. It will be easier to pull off if it's fun. You should already know who your preferred clients are so your guest list is set.

Please pick something that you think your clients will respond to. You might want to consider how you will ask your clients to your event.

Special stationary, email, phone invite, etc. This is about them. Make them feel special.

## Your Ideas

# STRATEGY #57

## CREATE JOINT VENTURES WITH OTHER COMPANIES PRODUCTS OR SERVICES*

Joint ventures (JV) are what could be one of your strongest strategies. A joint venture is when you work with another business to offer something to their clients that helps everyone involved. Consider it a partnership.

It helps your business because you get more exposure and hopefully a new client. It helps the business that offered your product or service because it gave something of value to their clients. Lastly it helped the client because they either wanted or needed the product or service that you offered them.

A true win-win-win. Something that we all as entrepreneurs and business people strive for.

Remember you are taking their clients and turning them into yours as well so please be respectful.

It also works the other way around. You can offer up your clients to someone else's business so that they can grow.

It is important that in either case, each business is satisfactorily benefited. It could be with a percentage of the sales which is common or with whatever means you can agree on.

## Here's an example:

A golf pro shop who offers high end golf clubs and accessories has struck a deal with the golf course around the corner from them. You get 2 FREE rounds of golf with every golf club set that is purchased.

The golf course is one of the nicest in the area so the value of the 2 FREE rounds of golf is $179 which is real money because that is what you would spend if you went there. The course is looking for new clients and the FREE golf gives the course the exposure they need and hopefully some sales in the restaurant and golf shop also.

The golf course would like more golfers because if a tee time passes and it isn't full with golfers then the course has lost revenue from that tee time. So the course gives the pro shop FREE passes to give away to their best clients knowing that if they've spent $700-1000 on new clubs they would be the golf courses target market for new clients.

The pro shop also wanted to give a great incentive to their clients for them to buy now that doesn't include dropping their prices and profit margins. The pro shop looks like the hero to their clients by giving them free golf. Besides when you buy new clubs, the first thing you want to do is hit golf balls with them.

## Call to Action:

Search out businesses that make sense to you and would make sense to your clients. In the example, I stayed within the same industry. This doesn't need to be the case.

You can search for items that your clients will purchase anyway like if you are a high end car dealer, a boat dealership would be a nice tie in. Or maybe a country club or a jewelry store. Go to where your clients already go.

Create your list and start contacting them. They need clients also. Make it a win-win-win and you can't go wrong. If the JV doesn't have your vision and can't see the opportunity then move on. Most people won't because this is a foreign idea to them.

If necessary, you can educate them if you really believe that they are the best fit for you.

# Your Ideas

# STRATEGY #58

# CREATE A MEMBERSHIP CLUB

Memberships can be a great business model. You can have an open membership club that lets everyone in or a private membership that has exclusive benefits.

The FREE model is good just to bring people in and build up your prospect list. Then you can sell them your product or service or a JV's product or service.

The private model has a dues component to it like a monthly, quarterly or yearly fee. You get exclusive content, information, offers, etc.

These clients will be your best and they will spend the most with you.

Sophisticated businesses have both so they can get the most out of their prospects and clients.

One last thing on the private memberships, you can have different levels of status like silver, gold and platinum that have different information and different monetary payments attached to them.

## Here's an example:

Dan Kennedy has a newsletter business, a consulting business, a seminar business and a copywriting business.

⬤ More Clients....More Often...More Money

He does his business through a membership structure that is essentially a gold, platinum and private coaching hierarchy.

Each of the three groups are on his newsletter list.

The Gold membership level gets his entry level newsletter and a modest discount to attend his seminars he holds. They also get lowest priority for copywriting and private coaching.

Platinum Membership gets the basic membership like the Gold but they also get some extra information that Gold doesn't and they get better discounts to seminars.

The Private membership levels get all of the above plus private one on one access to Dan.

Dan's plan is for everyone of his members to eventually ascend up in the membership ranks and become better clients. Better clients who make more money and spend more money with him.

## Call to Action:

I truly believe that any business can have a membership program. Every business has clients who are better than others.

What type of membership plan can you put together? What type of things can you offer to your members that are different from your regular clients?

Consider items can that can easily be scaled up like information or tangible products that can purchased or offered easily.

The last thing to offer and the most expensive item to offer is your time. Your time should be considered very valuable and only given out if you are paid well for your time.

**Your Ideas**

# PART 2 - SUMMARY

You just read about the different ways to bring your clients back to your business or website More Often.

Remember in Part One, you were trying to get new clients into your business. This was the next step in the process.

Are you starting to see the difference in your efforts and your thought processes?

Getting new clients to come into your business or visit your website is easier than getting those same clients to come back for a visit. You have to really work at that one.

I think you can see the value you will offer your clients with the strategies that you were just taught. I keep saying this so forgive the redundancy; this is about them and not you.

Zig Ziglar had a very famous quote that accurately describes what I have been writing about.

"You will get all you want in life, if you help enough other people get what they want."

Are you catching on a little more now? This is a lot of work but the rewards are unbelievable. I promise you that. Just keep doing it. Trust me.

Jim Gehrke

# Part Three

# More Money

The last part of "More Clients...More Often...More Money" is to have your clients spend more money with you.

If you remember the other two parts were about getting new clients and then getting them to come more often.

This is all about more money. Let's see if it excites you as much as it does me.

Also like the other two sections, take from this section what will make the most sense for you to implement first.

You will see some strategies that were also listed in sections one and two. Keep those in the front of your mind. They are very critical to your success in business. Implement them first.

Remember to takes great notes and think about how these strategies will look when placed into your business.

This step requires you to have the most trust built up with your clients. By now if you have been implementing along the way, you have made great strides with this and the process is working just like it should be.

I think you will find this part to be very exciting to you. Keep the creative juices flowing. You're doing great.

# STRATEGY #59

## DEVELOP IRRESISTIBLE OFFERS*

This may very well be the most important strategy. This has been listed in every section of the book. Irresistible offers give your clients a reason to spend their money with you.

An irresistible offer is an offer that is so good, so tempting that your client cannot possibly say "no". It's a way to build a stronger relationship together. A way to continue to build trust. You probably know this already but the public is very skeptical of everything these days.

Think of an irresistible offer as a welcomed bribe so that you can show just how wonderful you are.

Since by now you know what your lifetime value of a client is so you know what you can offer and not offer.

In case you haven't done this critical step you will need to know how many active clients you have, how much they spend on average and for how long they stay as a client. Remember, these are averages.

Let's say your business has 275 active clients who spends $200 per year and stays for four years. Multiply 275 x 200 x 4. What do those numbers tell you?

You bring in $55,000 per year and $220,000 over the four years. Each client is worth $800 to you as their lifetime value.

Now you will be able to better determine what your irresistible offer can be.

## Here's an example:

You want to start running. You think about going to the local running shoe store and buy a pair of running shoes off the rack. You go there and find a pair you like and then one of their staff comes up to you and starts asking you questions about what it is you are looking for.

In your mind, you already purchased the shoes you picked out but you play along with the sales clerk.

He asks you what your goals are, how long you will run for, where you will run, indoor or outdoor, how your feet are, etc...

This expert consultation gives you more knowledge about running that you ever thought was necessary. You quickly realized that the shoes you had picked out will not meet your needs but the shoes that are a perfect match for you are much more expensive and out of your budget.

Most people would leave and have to think about it because they wouldn't want to buy the inferior product now; that would embarrass them. The expert has an irresistible offer for their new client that he can pass along. He understands the new shoes are much more expensive and that he has given the new client so much information and education that any other shoe wouldn't do.

The store has an irresistible offer for new clients/leads where you get a shoe fitting for free ($49 value), you are tested on their treadmill to see your running form ($97 value), you will get a free membership to their running group which is perfect for you to continue your momentum into running and develop new friendships and you will also get a 15% discount on the shoes you will purchase that day.

The client has an offer they can't refuse. They spent more than they expected but they found a new home for all things running. Someone who wants the best for them... Someone who wants them to keep coming back time and again because they have taken the time to educate them. They were also educated on a new area of interest to them and they realized what they didn't know would hurt them.

## Call to Action:

First and foremost, figure out what your lifetime value of a client is. This number will dictate what you can and cannot do going forward as a business.

Once you have your lifetime value number you can write down what you can give away to get your clients to spend more money with you. Also write down what you can't do or give away. This is a creative exercise.

When you create your irresistible offer, you will need to ask yourself if it's good enough to get your clients to come back to spend more money.

Remember your offer can include bonuses like a FREE class or FREE report. It doesn't have to only be discounts. You have lots of options. Maybe it includes FREE stuff from a partnering business. Who knows until you start writing stuff on paper.

## Your Ideas

# STRATEGY #60

## OFFER STRONG GUARANTEES*

Guarantees allow for clients to purchase with peace of mind knowing they can always get taken care of with any problem that may arise. Offering strong guarantees is the best way to continue your relationship.

The longer the guarantee the more comfortable your client is. Craftsman tools have a lifetime guarantee. I have a few of them because of the guarantee alone. Lifetime is the best guarantee you can offer.

Guarantees and return policies scare business owners. They think the public will take advantage of them with this type of guarantee. This is bad thinking.

How many times have you returned something the last day you could because the receipt said you had 10 days to do it by? I know I have.

If that business would've put a longer time on the receipt I probably would've kept it because I would have forgotten about the return policy.

Do not let a couple of your clients who may abuse your return policies or your guarantees let you dictate a bad business decision.

They really aren't your clients anyway. They're probably cherry pickers and you shouldn't waste your time with them.

## Here's an example:

The local auto mechanic offers a spring tune-up for $99. This is a good deal for everyone involved. Good deal for the auto mechanic, good deal for the clients and a good deal for your car.

What the mechanic also offers is that, if for any reason your car has mechanical issues related to the tune-up within 90 days of service, we will service your car for FREE. Now that is a great guarantee.

Current clients appreciate the fact that your mechanic takes pride in their work and offers you a great deal. .

## Call to Action:

How long of a guarantee can you offer? How strong of a guarantee can you offer? Write down what you can do and what it would look like if you doubled it.

What does that mean by doubling it? Can you extend your warranty or guarantee by twice as much time? Two years instead of One? Can you offer double your money back if not completely satisfied?

Interesting questions aren't they? Does it Get you thinking? How many of my clients would actually take me up on my guarantee? 1%, 5%, 10% or more?

It's been proven over and over and in every possible industry. The stronger your guarantee, return policy or warranty you offer the more sales you will enjoy and the less return percentage you will have.

I am assuming of course that you offer a quality product or service and that you are not a conman.

## Your Ideas

# STRATEGY #61

## PACKAGE COMPLIMENTARY PRODUCTS OR SERVICES TOGETHER (BUNDLING)

I've had you thinking about your business a lot in this book. In this section you will get a ton more ideas on how to offer different packages.

This is one of those strategies. Packaging complimentary products or services is very easy. I'll give you several examples to show just how easy this is.

If you sell shoes, include socks. If you sell golf bags, include shoes. If you sell internet marketing, include email marketing. If you sell tennis racquets, include tennis shoes. If you sell yarn, include knitting needles.

Do you get the idea?

## Here's an example:

We get a lawn service every year. We don't have anyone cut the grass for us (bummer) but we do have our lawn treated for weeds.

This is a common practice every spring and summer pretty much everywhere in the country.

The company we have has other services they offer. They have fertilizers and winterizing products as well as aerating of the lawn in the fall.

They package these services together to make it very attractive to their clients to choose a more inclusive product to take care of their lawns so they look fantastic.

## Call to Action:

I'm guessing by now you have some options you can offer your clients. In fact you may have been doing this strategy already.

It's simple to do.

This strategy is also very easy to do as a suggestive sell by your staff at the checkout counter. Remember back to your employees being trained in sales?

In fact you may consider offering new products and services just to package things together.

## Your Ideas

# STRATEGY #62

## DEVELOP POINT OF SALE PROMOTIONS

Point of sale promotions are what you might see at a grocery store or gas station checkout counter with a sign like "three doughnuts for a $1.00".

It is also an interactive kiosk you might find in a Home Depot or other large store educating you with a video on their products.

Funny how education comes back into the mix with this strategy.

This strategy lends itself to impulse sales whether it is in a retail store or online. Most successful point of sale purchases.

### Here's an example:

There's a gas station I like to go to that always has something inexpensive on sale at the checkout counter.

It is only one item per day so they switch it up on a daily basis. It's also an item that every clerk asks their clients if they would want at the point of sale.

It's very effective, it's an impulse and it's always an attractive price. It's never an expensive item.

They get it. And they're good at it. This simple strategy makes them millions in sales.

## Call to Action:

If you have a retail store or a professional service; what can you put at the counter to attract an impulse sale.

Please do not discount these incidental sales as insignificant. If you have tight margins, these sales can make or break your business.

If you are online, is there something you can offer for sale to your clients after they decided to purchase from you?

What I mean is that there has been proven statistics that show an online purchaser is something like 40% likely to purchase a second item from you if you offer them a discounted item to go along with what they just bought.

This is as easy as you want it to be. You don't have to over complicate things.

## Your Ideas

# STRATEGY #63

## OFFER LARGER UNITS OF SALE (BULK)

Larger units are what Costco and Sam's Club was built around. If you need six ketchups instead of one, they are your destination place.

Why buy one spool of thread when two is better. How about a pitcher of beer instead of a pint? Purchase six socks instead of one.

I think you get the idea.

This is a simple one to create for your clients because almost anything can be multiplied or bulked up.

### Here's an example:

I mentioned Costco and Sam's club above. They are the King's of larger unit sales. They didn't invent the practice but they perfected it.

We shop at Sam's club for our party supplies. There's nothing that says a party like a 5# bag of Chex Mix.

In fact they have perfected this process so well that they have larger units called "institutional sized" now in multiple packaging so their larger units are now bulked up. So this means you can purchase a bundled package of two institutional sized items together.

Bigger can be better.

## Call to Action:

What can you put together to allow your clients to buy more of something? You may be surprised at what it is that your clients would buy.

My theory is that this is a test. Remember testing things in the beginning of this book?

Try something out and offer it to your clients. Email them or put it in your sale flyer or make an impulse type sign.

There is no losing here. If your clients don't want it no big deal, just move on to another offer.

One more thing the reverse also works. If you have to purchase or buy in a large amount; a smaller unit of sale might be an answer for you to test.

## Your Ideas

# STRATEGY #64

## CHANGE THE LANGUAGE OR DESCRIPTION OF YOUR PRODUCTS OR SERVICES SO THEY SEEM MORE UPSCALE*

This might confuse you at first. It did me. Companies have changed the names and descriptions of products and services for decades.

Sometimes they need to be updated with a fresh look and name. Car companies do this all the time. They take the same chassis and replace it with a new body style.

Sometimes car companies share the same car and rename it to sell it to a different audience.

Does anyone remember the Chrysler LeBaron and the Mazzerati Chrysler? Same looking car but one had the Chrysler logo and sold for less and the other had the Mazzerati logo and sold for a lot more. To be fair it did have nicer equipment.

### Here's an example:

Have you ever eaten Grouper? It's a fish. Maybe you know it by a different name; Chilean Sea Bass.

Confused? Nobody wanted Grouper. Everyone wanted Chilean Sea Bass at twice the price.

This is a classic example of a name change that really helped the fishing industry. Fisherman knew how good Grouper tasted if they could only get the public to try it, they would be set.

Well the public never warmed up to the name and they decided to change it. The rest as they say is bon appétit.

## Call to Action:

Do you have a product that you manufacture or sell that is a dog? Is there something that just won't move off the shelves? How about an online tool that sounds complicated for the general public to grasp?

Have fun and test out some name changes to see if the new identity you give your product or service is more appealing.

Think of foreign names. Italian and Latin are always popular.

Also consider thinking in terms of features and benefits to rename your product.

You will never know where genius will come from.

## Your Ideas

# STRATEGY #65

# DEVELOP UP-SELLS

Up-sells are the art of creating sales just by asking. More specifically it is the art of selling your client a better product than the one they were looking at.

You've had car dealers do this to you every time you've bought a car. You may have had your florist do the same thing to you.

Up-sells are money makers for businesses. They take the average sale and make it into a better or terrific sale.

Most clients of yours know they need something when they come into your store. They start by looking at price and then functionality.

After that it's anyone's guess what they will decide upon.

Go back to where I teach you about Sales training for your staff. That is priceless to you because up-sells are the goose that lays the golden eggs along with its cousin cross-sells which is next.

## Here's an example:

You go into a high end watch seller. It's usually a jewelry store. They are masters at tweaking your wallet and ego.

You have a budget of $2500 and you are there for a brand new Rolex because you have always wanted one and you are finally at a place in life where you can justify the expenditure.

The sales rep asks you some basic questions like your budget, the styles you like, what type of work you do, etc.

You find the best watch you could in the price range you stated. Your happy.

Now comes the up-sell. The master sales professional wants to show you a brand new Rolex that just came in. No one in the area owns this watch. It's just gorgeous.

It's also another $2500 or double your budget. You look at the watch and you fall in love instantly but you know that it's too much money.

The sales professional gently reminds you that with your stature at the firm you're at, you will be taken more seriously, looked at differently, clients will respect you more which will all equate to more money for you in the end.

You will be more successful as a result of this new high end Rolex. This sales professional has justified the extra expense and you agree.

You buy the more expensive Rolex and you feel like a million bucks. Win-Win

Yes... it's that easy.

## Call to Action:

Do you offer multiple products of the same type of product? Let's say you have pens for sale; are there multiple kinds for your clients to consider?

Maybe something at 50¢, $1.50, $5.75 and $225.00 just to mix things up.

You don't have to put the example above in "stone", it's just something to consider.

But at the same time it's important to have options for your clients. Hopefully you have them. Most businesses offer three different products. A low, middle and high end item.

Start there at the very least if it's practical for you to do so.

Then go back to the strategy of training your staff on how to be a salesperson and train them again on how to sell the higher end products you offer. It will benefit you greatly as a business owner.

# Your Ideas

# STRATEGY #66

## DEVELOP CROSS-SELLS

Cross-sells are the cousin of Up-sells because they are similar but different. They are easier to sell than up-sells because they are easier for your clients to grasp its need.

This strategy is where you suggest a complimentary product to what your client is purchasing. If your client is buying charcoal for their grills, you would offer charcoal fluid as a product that they might need also.

You could take it a step further and also suggest a grill pan that is for making pizzas or grilled vegetables on your clients grill too.

Do you notice the subtle difference between Cross-sells and Up-sells? An up-sell in that grilling example would be to suggest using a mesquite wood chip instead of charcoal.

Make no mistake about it, this is gold to your cash register or online merchant account. This can literally make or break your bottom line.

### Here's an example:

There's a joke amongst us that goes something like "if you don't get a college education the only thing you'll need to know is *Would You Like Fries With That?*"

It may be a bad joke but you've probably have heard it more than once.

Well the expression *"Would You Like Fries With That?"* is a cross-sell. Fast food companies are making millions by training their staffs to offer something extra when a client of theirs comes to the counter or goes through a drive-thru.

Remember the "value meal, meal deal or super size expressions"? All cross-sells.

If they can do it, you can do it.

## Call to Action:

This shouldn't be too difficult. What do you have to offer that compliments what your clients are buying?

This will be important for your staff to know your products and the uses of those products.

Most clients will be open to you suggesting complimentary products because most of the time they don't know complimentary products exist or they may not remember they need that product.

You are doing your clients a huge service by suggesting cross-sells. You just have to embrace it as a concept.

Hopefully you see the value in this strategy. This may help; some people call this "add-on" sales.

## Your Ideas

# STRATEGY #67

## DEVELOP MONTHLY CONTINUITY*

How would you like your bank accounts filled up with money every first of the month? You Do? I thought you might.

Continuity is the way to do that. Think about car loans, membership fees, health clubs, etc.

Think continuous when you talk about continuity. Continuous money coming into your business is good.

Almost every business can implement this income stream. It's smart business if you can start it.

Health clubs are a simple example of continuity. On the first of each month they draw money out of your bank account "x" number of dollars whether you use the facility or not.

They are banking on the fact that you won't use the facility that much and you won't cancel your account anytime soon.

Think about every bill you pay each month. Some services you use and some you are paying for no good reason at all.

Isn't continuity great?

## Here's an example:

As good as health clubs are, there are also great business models you can model yourselves after.

Paid newsletters come to mind. I have subscribed for years to Dan Kennedy's marketing newsletter.

I mentioned earlier about Dan Kennedy. He's a genius and his newsletter is worth every penny I spend.

He has built up his newsletter over the years to what it is now but I want you to think about these numbers:

25,000 subscribers paying $40-60 per month for the newsletter. A bunch of those subscribers have signed up for his next level of membership of $249 per month

Not sure if you've done the math or not but he is at 1-1.5 million per month in continuity income.

Not too shabby.

Plus he brings in experts from fields of marketing that he is not an expert in. They do it for the exposure and he does it to offer more knowledge.

Any remember JV's and Strategic Alliances from earlier in the book?

## Call to Action:

What can you do that your clients would pay a monthly fee for?

This is a creative exercise so write down options for yourself. If you have a consumable like food and drink you can offer something like get $40 of food and drink for $30 per month plus you'll get member only benefits that no one else will be able to enjoy.

That ties a client in to coming to your store each and every month and not your competitor. That is just one example that can be mixed and matched with other industries.

To make this worthwhile to you and your clients, your offer will have to be good. If it is just ok then only your hard core best clients will take you up on it because they are probably spending it now anyway.

Remember back to the irresistible offer you created earlier in this book.

# Your Ideas

# STRATEGY #68

## CLOSING THE SALE

There's an old saying in the sales world; "Always Be Closing". ABC for short.

What that means is that you look at every client and prospect as someone you want to sell your products and services to.

It also means that when talking to a client you are leading them along a path to purchase the products or services you offer.

The fatal flaw of so many sales people is not asking for the sale. They are great at educating and leading their prospects down the path to making a buying decision but then fall short at the close.

I have mentioned sales all along in this book because as I mentioned earlier; everyone in your company is in sales. They are representing your company every time they have an interaction with the public.

Closing the sale will give your bottom line a huge boost. This is one of those strategies that you really need to implement in your business. It's that important.

### Here's an example:

I mentioned that a lot of sales people are great at educating and leading a buyer along a sales path but don't close. That was me.

Way back in the day I sold insurance. I wasn't any good at it but I sold it once in a while.

My mistake was not asking for the sale. I was taught a 53 page script that followed my prospect along the sales path. While the script was incredible at educating and showing need, it was weak at closing.

Since I didn't know any better I didn't know this at the time. My prospects were always left off the hook in making a buying decision. I thought I was doing everything right. I wasn't.

I left the company after three years not knowing what I was doing wrong.

It didn't take long for me to realize my mistakes when I went for training on sales techniques. I never asked for the sale. Not in the way I should've anyway.

## Call to Action:

Learning to close the sale is about asking some simple but important questions. It's all about getting your prospect to "own" the product.

I'll give you some examples:

--"would you like the red one or the blue one?"

--"would you prefer Tuesday's or Thursday's for delivery?"

--"what jeans fit you the best?"

--"how would you like to pay for this? cash, store charge or something else?"

If your prospects answer these questions, they have already mentally bought. It's because your prospects will always give you buying signals.

You need to pay attention to their body language and the words they use.

What questions can you come up with that will help you close more sales?

They don't have to be clever. Sometimes the simplest ones are the best.

## Your Ideas

# STRATEGY #69

## RAISING YOUR PRICES

Yes, I said to raise your prices. It really can be this simple. Every company in the world is trying to be the cheapest. I don't want you to be like them.

I think they're idiots to be blunt about it. Here's why:

1. It is unsustainable.
2. It hurts the marketplace more than it helps because it de-values everything.
3. With small margins, how can employees expect to get paid well.
4. If your clients always want the cheapest pricing there will be no loyalty.
5. You have to do more sales volume.
6. You have turned your business into a commodity instead of special.

I hope you are starting to see the picture of why this is a bad thing. Now with that all said, sales and promotions do not apply. They are still a vital tactic to use. I'm referring to a business philosophy where this is an everyday practice and business model.

So why should you raise your prices?

Honestly, you are probably too cheap. You don't value your products and services and you think your clients are always looking for a bargain and come to you to get one.

I hope this book has taught you that if you implement the strategies in these pages, you will have such a loyal client base that they will gladly pay a little extra just to be a part of something special. You are that "special".

I'm not saying to double all of your prices. Your clients will not understand why you are doing it and if you haven't built up that loyalty they will leave you.

Start with 5% or maybe 10% especially if it is a non-competitively priced item. Most clients will not notice a modest price increase.

I know raising your prices are scary and that fear stops you in your tracks. But keep in mind that it is your fear, not your clients. I'm willing to bet you that you will lose no clients because of this and your bank account will thank you on a monthly basis.

## Here's an example:

One of the first years of my Putting Green business I put out an outrageous offer of $6 per square foot for a custom Putting Green.

I was selling strictly on price and not on value. I didn't value what I offered and I had doubts about myself and my abilities to create a custom Putting Green.

If I had those doubts then why wouldn't my clients have those doubts too? They do if you let them have those doubts.

I got a lot of business because of this low pricing which didn't surprise me. I also gave up a ton of profit which would have helped me grow my business much quicker.

Lessons learned and now after 15 years, I don't have doubts about my business or my pricing or about me anymore.

There was something very interesting I learned after I raised my prices the next year. No one told me that I wasn't worth it. No one told me I was too expensive because of the price increase. It was all in my head and what I thought of myself.

And the bottom line is this; because of the price increases over the years I have been able to go on very nice vacations with my wife. I have played some of the best golf courses in the world and I have grown my business each and every year.

## Call to Action:

What's the first thing you can raise your prices on? Maybe it's something as simple as an extra 10¢ or 50¢ or even several dollars.

Every little bit will help your bottom line.

If you have been implementing the strategies in this book along the way you have already seen the growth in your business and how your clients are responding to the changes.

Raising your prices will also allow you to offer better sales and promotions down the road if you choose to offer a discounted price.

Just keep in mind that any increase you put into action is all profit. You were willing to sell an item at "X" and now you have it priced at "Y" for more.

I know it's scary but it needs to be done. Think about this; how many more clients do you need to come through your doors or visit your website for you to make an extra $1000?

What if you did nothing but raise your prices? How long would it take to earn that same $1000 if you didn't get any new clients? The answer will surprise you.

## Your Ideas

# STRATEGY #70

## LOWERING YOUR OVERHEAD

To be honest I didn't want to add this in. There isn't a sales growth aspect to this strategy. It's all about cutting costs.

Now don't get me wrong, cutting costs is important especially if there is an area where your expenses are way out of whack.

This whole book however will increase your expenses not decrease them. What this book will do for you is; it will double, triple or increase your sales so high that the increased expenses won't matter.

That is why you will hear the truly successful people say *that is an invest of "X" not an expense of "X"*. They really don't look at things like expenses. They look at what the results or benefits will be.

Anyway, getting back to lowering your overhead is as simple as cutting payroll, looking for less expensive vendors, finding a better accountant who can depreciate or write off more business expenses, etc.

I think lowering overhead is an inherent skill everyone has because of how they run their own personal expenses and budget.

Just don't cut overhead to cut overhead. Have a well thought out plan in place.

## Here's an example:

There is a local manufacturer who makes engines for garden equipment like lawn mowers. They only run two shifts now. They used to run three.

They have figured out a way to keep the building at full capacity which helps their bottom line.

They found a start-up company who couldn't afford their own machines or building. So what they did was to lease their equipment and building to this start-up for one eight hour period every day.

So, the shift that wasn't needed anymore was now being used by this start-up who were building non-competing engines. Pretty slick right?

It was a way to lower overhead because they were paying for the building and machines anyway. Now they were generating revenue without being there. Another great win-win.

This is the kind of lowering overhead that I fully support. Not the slash and burn that so many companies do.

## Call to Action:

What do you have that a smaller company could lease temporarily or permanently? It could be something as simple as an office.

This strategy is perfect for printers, engineering firms, gyms, etc. Any place that has expensive items that someone small might not be able to afford.

I have a friend who rented an expensive piece of engineering equipment that he couldn't afford to buy. It worked great for both parties because it wasn't something that gave away any confidential information to my friend about any of their clients. Win-win

If you think about this strategy, I bet you have something to offer. If you don't, no big deal.

## Your Ideas

_____

_____

_____

_____

_____

_____

_____

_____

_____

_____

_____

_____

_____

_____

_____

_____

# PART 3 - SUMMARY

As you read, money isn't a bad thing. It's actually good. It doesn't make you happy, that comes from within but it makes everything easier. Easier to grow your business, pay your bills and allow you to breathe a little easier.

You read some very important but some very simple strategies to implement into your business. How many are you already doing? How many can you start today?

Did you notice that there were strategies that were in this section also? Remember if you see a strategy repeated, you can count on it being critical to your success. It's a strategy you can build on and grow on.

Business doesn't have to be so hard. It just needs a little thought on how to do it better.

Too many business owners are going through their daily routines being busy. They are not focusing on the important things like growing their businesses.

I know that sounds crazy but think about it. When was the last time you sat down to have a strategy session on growing your business? How about one to put out fires? Yeah, those come all of the time.

Growing your business should be more pressing than putting out fires. It's a hell of a lot more fun too.

# Conclusion

## WOW!!!!

I hope you saw the real potential of your business. If you didn't then I failed you somewhere along the way.

The information you just read WILL transform your business. It WILL change your life. It WILL blow away any and all competition you have.

I want to personally thank you for getting to this point of the book. It's means that you care about your business enough to make it as important to you as your family is.

It also means that we connected along the way. Maybe it was the strategies I put in this book or maybe it was the way I write. I thank you from the bottom of my soul. It means the world to me.

As my way of saying thanks, I want to offer you a FREE Quick Start Guide that will help you get started. I'm also going to invite you to attend a FREE webinar that is meant to go together with the Quick Start Guide.

These two tools are meant to help you get going or to get you unstuck if you have hit a road block. It isn't unusual for either of these two circumstances to occur.

So what should you do next? If you haven't started yet I'm going to give you what I think is the "Top 10" strategies to implement first. They may not be the easiest but they will leverage your time and your money the quickest and be the best use of your time.

1) Develop Irresistible Offers

2) Develop Your Unique Selling Proposition (USP)

3) Create Referral Systems

4) Create Joint Ventures

5) Develop Strategic Alliances

6) Develop Up-sells

7) Develop Cross-sells

8) Develop Monthly Continuity

9) Develop a Back-end of Products or Services

10) Create a Follow-up Sales/Marketing   Funnel

This list is no particular order. You can put your own order to it because there is no wrong order.

Each one is just as valuable as the other.

This will be an exciting journey you're about to go on. I remember going on this journey a few years ago and I was excited.

Mind you I didn't have all of these strategies laid out for me. I had to create a lot of these on my own. You are definitely at an advantage over me but none the less at a point where all you can do is grow.

You will grow as a business owner and grow as a person. You are in the "Pole Position" so to speak.

Best of luck. I know you'll be great. Enjoy the ride. Now get to it.

# CONTINUING EDUCATION

It is surprising how many people think that when they are done with school; learning stops. Let me clear this up for you; it's just beginning.

This book is continuing education. You read this to learn something you didn't already know. Maybe you were looking for one little tidbit of information that would take your business to the next level. Maybe you are beginning in business and were looking for a road map of sorts on how to proceed.

Learning is lifelong. Education is power, it's strength, it's confidence.

I have spent 10 times as much money on my personal education in the business world than I did on my college education. I didn't write that to brag. I knew that I needed to be better at what I was doing and I got the training and education that put me in a better position to help me attain my goals.

Now I challenge you to continue on with your education. I have created a "Quick Start Guide and Webinar" for you to get the most value out of this book than you possibly can.

I know for some of you this will be intellectual entertainment and nothing else. I get that. I've done it myself from time to time. But for those who truly want their business to be different; this is the place.

I really want you to go to:

MoreClientsMoreOftenMoreMoney.com

and continue your education. Watch the webinar, read the blog posts, sign-up for the newsletter, get involved if you wish. Let's start a relationship together if you like what you've read in this book and feel I can help. I'm all in, are you?

Jim Gehrke

# Meet The Author

Jim Gehrke is a serial entrepreneur. He has profitably owned six different businesses and he wants to bring his knowledge and experiences to you. His experiences cover dozens of industries so pick up this book and learn from Jim's many successes (and failures).

He has been married to his beautiful bride Kris since 1991 and he looks forward to growing very old with her.

In his spare time he loves to play golf, drink a little wine and try new beers. He also enjoys listening to music, laughing with friends and traveling.

Over the last couple of years, he has become a decent cook with just enough knowledge to be dangerous to those who eat his food.

Jim has found his passion when it comes to helping businesses grow. He loves to create strategy for a business owner and see that plan implemented and become successful. Nothing makes him happier.